Praise for *Kickass R*

"Billy Manas thoughtfully draws from his own powerful story of addiction and recovery to extend encouragement, courage, and hope to others. He compassionately invites readers to remember the context in which addiction happens, and offers an empowering lens through which readers can recognize how the strengths they already possess will serve them well on their journey of recovery."
— **Holly Parker, PhD,** author of *When Reality Bites: How Denial Helps and What to Do When It Hurts*

"Billy Manas makes getting clean and sober a helluva lot cooler and more freeing than staying hot and messy any day!"
— **Tania Katan,** author of *Creative Trespassing*

"Billy Manas's debut book, *Kickass Recovery*, is an authentic and needed testament to the power of recovering out loud. His honest, empowering, and sincere story will surely lead readers to the conclusion that anyone can find purpose through overcoming pain and adversity."
— **Ryan Hampton,** advocate and author of *American Fix: Inside the Opioid Addiction Crisis — and How to End It*

"What do you get when you marry powerful memoir with smart self-help? *Kickass Recovery*! You won't find a better book on how *you* can create a recovery program that really works than *Kickass Recovery*. Highly recommended!"
— **Eric Maisel,** coauthor of *Creative Recovery: A Complete Addiction Treatment Program That Uses Your Natural Creativity*

"The secret to overcoming addiction is not getting off drugs but *staying* off drugs and getting a life. This book describes one man's journey to do just that. While Billy Manas's story is unique and personal, the lessons are universal and can be shared. This book suggests that there is power in positive thinking and that life tends to be a self-fulfilling prophesy. But ultimately, it shows that if you want things in your life to turn out differently, you have to do them differently."

— **Walter Ling, MD,** author of *Mastering the Addicted Brain* and professor emeritus of psychiatry, David Geffen School of Medicine, UCLA

KICKASS
RECOVERY

KICKASS
RECOVERY

FROM YOUR FIRST YEAR CLEAN
TO THE LIFE OF YOUR DREAMS

BILLY MANAS

Foreword by Liberty DeVitto

New World Library
Novato, California

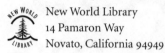 New World Library
14 Pamaron Way
Novato, California 94949

Text design by Tona Pearce Myers

Library of Congress Cataloging-in-Publication data is available.

First printing, March 2020
ISBN 978-1-60868-650-6
Ebook ISBN 978-1-60868-651-3
Printed in Canada on 100% postconsumer-waste recycled paper

 New World Library is proud to be a Gold Certified Environmentally Responsible Publisher. Publisher certification awarded by Green Press Initiative.

10   9   8   7   6   5   4   3   2   1

*For Bella, Gloria, and River — you guys are the light,
the moon, and the stars…*

Contents

Part 3: Kick Ass

Foreword

Billy Manas hits a high note with *Kickass Recovery*. For thirty years, I played drums for and partied with some of the biggest names in the rock world. When the bubble burst and I was thrust out of the spotlight, I was lost. My friends were gone, and my music had died. It wasn't easy to accept the fact that I was a drummer without a band, and before long, my best friend became a bottle.

As Billy says, recovery is great, but it's easy to hide in the meetings. I found myself doing just that. Initially, going into bars or restaurants with friends who'd be drinking was pretty much out of the question. I was faced with knowing I needed to learn how to get back to doing what I was born to do — play the drums — and do it as a sober person. It was quite an adjustment.

We all know how important recovery is — especially these days, with drugs and alcohol running so rampant — and a book like *Kickass Recovery* can take a lot of the mystery out of not only living sober but living the life of your dreams.

Your life is out there. Whether you want to drive a truck or be a musician or an artist or maybe just fall in love and start a family — it's all available to you if you know how to get it.

Through the grace of God, I now have a beautiful family, and my career as a musician continues to live on even today. The difference is, this time I am sober.

To the sober life and living free,
Liberty DeVitto
Drums, Billy Joel, 1974–2003

Introduction

My moment of clarity came when I was sitting on the stoop of a Hudson Valley bakery at about 7 AM. I was a hot mess — high and drunk — and the only thing that shone clearly through my haze was the undeniable fact that I was at the end of my rope. I had been going through an endless cycle of emergency-room visits followed by hospital admittances all summer. And as much as I wanted to believe it was simply a temporary illness, a voice inside me kept reminding me that it was not normal for a forty-year-old's endocrine system to be "shutting down," as the doctors had explained it.

At that very moment, I watched a happy young family get out of their Volvo wagon to go enjoy an early breakfast in Rosendale. The mom was blonde and in perfect physical shape, the dad looked like he just stepped out of an L.L. Bean catalog, and the kids were cute. They radiated a feeling of positivity that I'd only ever noticed from afar. As I watched them walk past me — carefully leaving enough space so that they wouldn't catch whatever they thought I was infected with — it occurred to me that my substance abuse shut me out of the life they were currently basking in. I was forty years old. I had never made more than $350 per week. I was alone. I was a puddle of various addictions. The road I was on had no exits, and I was getting really damn close to the end of it.

Today I have over nine years clean and my own little family that I take out to breakfast — in my brand-new car. As I sit here writing this, I earn three times what I used to make. I have an awesome credit rating. And I am pursuing a career path I never would have allowed myself to imagine when I was sitting there on the stoop that day.

When I was an addict, it was a pretty common — even daily — experience to wake up with thirty-seven cents in my pocket. But somehow I could venture out and come back home three hours later with fifty dollars' worth of drugs, enough ramen noodles to feed me for the day, a ten-dollar pack of cigarettes, and a cup of coffee — all without breaking any laws (mostly). For addicts and alcoholics, the ability to scrape together an existence with little more than a few coins is a point of pride — the thrill of surviving despite a lack of resources creates a secondary addiction. If you are reading this, you probably know what I mean. I know you have stories that would rival Jesus's trick with the loaves and fishes. I know you've got the skills. In this book, I'm going to show you how to harness all those street smarts and that creativity to design a life beyond your wildest dreams.

Since I've been clean, I've spoken to thousands of other addicts in jails and church basements. The most common thing they tell me is that they knew they had to get clean, but living that way just seemed so boring — this, from people in bright-orange jumpsuits! I wrote this book to show you how a life of recovery can be ten times as exciting and a hundred times more fun than a life of active addiction. And in our current state, with the opioid epidemic and overdose deaths reaching record numbers, the time for recovery is *now*!

We'll discuss the various ways you can "get out of your own way" and create a life that you will totally fall in love with. We'll touch on gratitude and meditation, and even the more practical mechanics of how to make your dreams come true — everything from goal setting to exercises on how to find your calling and how to steer clear of the people who will try to take the air out of your tires (so to speak).

So, follow me: things are about to get real interesting.

PART

1

KICK OUT YOUR OLD
WAY OF THINKING

CHAPTER ONE

Flip On the Light

I'm going to get real with you. Whether you have one day clean, one month clean, or one year clean, you are doing great right now. In fact, chances are that if you are sitting down and reading this, you're not obsessing about copping or using. How do I know? Because reading and writing are my lifeblood, but when I'm in the grips of my addiction, I cannot even think about sitting down long enough to read *anything*. So right off the bat, you have every reason to be proud of yourself right now. At this exact moment.

Let me take a minute and give you a brief look into my story and how I went from the kid who was going to "grow up to be a brain surgeon" to a garden-variety junkie, because this story might remind you of who you were before you got into this mess, too. Let's face it: when we were lining up single file in first grade to go out to the playground after lunch, none of us imagined we'd be sticking needles in our arms, being rushed to the ER twice a month, or spending the night in Central Booking.

Congratulate Yourself

We have all been to meetings where a newcomer will show up with an air of uncertainty or talking some bullshit about wanting to get clean for his kids or his wife or his mother. It hardly ever works. Getting sober one day at a time is uncomfortable, difficult, and very close to impossible at first. This is obviously the reason why we call each other miracles when we see each other at meetings. It really is miraculous when we learn how to live clean.

This makes *you* a miracle. I'm guessing there was some pretty messed-up stuff that got you using in the first place, and you survived that. You also survived the hell of addiction. And now you've gone and gotten yourself clean. Do you know what a big fucking achievement that is?

So, first and foremost, congratulate yourself. Congratulate yourself for becoming an addict or an alcoholic, because you started using in the first place to protect yourself and keep yourself alive. It was a coping mechanism. And because you're still alive, it worked. It may not have worked efficiently or particularly gracefully, but it did work. Let's be honest: you'd more than likely be dead if you had not had that defense mechanism to get you through whatever it was you were being hurt by.

Then congratulate yourself for getting clean and finding a new way to live. And congratulate yourself for picking up this book and deciding that now is the time to rock your recovery!

Finally, congratulate yourself for having put yourself through an experience (addiction) where you learned exactly what you need to know to create a happy, fulfilling, successful life for yourself. You may not realize it yet, but all those scrappy, creative, so-crazy-it-just-might-work skills you used to get through another day "out there" also work in here. It's really just a matter of making a few well-thought-out adjustments. That's exactly what this book will teach you: how to channel all the skills you developed as an addict into creating a life that makes you feel good — *really* good, insanely good — with no mind-altering substances required.

Taking a Peek at the Past Helps You Create a Better Future

In many ways, recovery is about finding new coping mechanisms. But if you don't know what you need help coping *with*, or why these things make you feel like you have to cope in the first place, you're flying blind. For nearly everyone in recovery, there is constant noise in your head — and it's that noise that you were trying to drown out with substances.

What you may not realize is that the noise is the result of childhood baggage. Even though you're grown now and those threats don't exist anymore, the thought processes and coping mechanisms you developed as a response to them are still running the show. Meaning, you've been spending all that energy and ingesting all those substances to chase away uncomfortable entities that no longer exist.

The best way to break free from the past is to face it — just like when you were a kid the best way to stop being scared of the monster in your closet was to turn on the light. In this chapter, I'll help you flip that switch — and hold your hand. When you realize that the thing you've been running from is a shirt that can't hurt you, you'll be free of your fear. And that is the ultimate high!

I'll Go First

Do you know why you became addicted to whatever it was you were addicted to? No, the *real* reason why? I'm going to guide you through the process of getting an objective look at the things that got you addicted in the first place, but first I'll tell you my story. Hopefully it will trigger some insights into your own experiences that will help things go more smoothly when it's your turn in just a few pages.

As I share my story, feel free to nod and chuckle, just like we all do in those damp and gross church basements where we are reunited with our reason for living.

I was born in 1970, and I grew up on Long Island. My parents were fucking nuts (are you nodding yet?). Somehow — and this is just my theory — my father believed that moving to a new house in a new town every single year would result in his having cash on hand at all times. I'm not entirely sure what he was doing, but I suspect that he had some scheme where he would squeeze a little equity out of every situation — whether it was $7 or $8,000. My dad was known for the sort-of-illegal (but not enough to be jailed) fashion in which he navigated his life. Leasing cars under his dead father's name and social security number, rolling back the odometer on these leased cars, and most likely a dozen other tricks that I had no knowledge of were all game. My mom, on the other hand, had the most violent emotional highs and lows I've ever seen. A disagreement with a neighbor and she'd be outside hammering a "For Sale" sign into the lawn; an argument with my dad and she'd be screaming about how she was going to get a divorce, and then run into her room and cry. And it was not the sort of stifled weeping you'd hear from the ladies at church. It was always a very scary and guttural type of crying you might see at the scene of a fatal car wreck. This was a weekly occurrence.

Criminal dad and hysterical mom aside, always being new in the neighborhood — plus having a strange older brother with behavioral issues — meant that I invariably spent a lot of time by myself.

I actually had two older brothers — one three years older and the other two years older. The middle child, as is apt to happen, was the one with all the social issues. The prevailing theory the whole family held was that not being the oldest or youngest made him feel a lack of identity that led to his obvious need for negative attention. Whatever the case may be, if some weird and distasteful bullshit was going on, he was always steering the ship.

One of my favorite parts of my middle brother's repertoire — and, yes, I am being sarcastic — was his penchant for sitting in the cafeteria alone for hours with his head down telling anyone who would listen that he was going to kill himself. This was always very helpful when you were new at a school.

It was super difficult to impress the ladies when you became known as the Addams Family within the first week of living anywhere, but male friends — that was a disaster all its own. The typical pattern was for me to try to befriend someone who'd lived on the block since he was born. This usually took place in the weeks preceding the complimentary nicknames like the Addams Family. It would always start with me making a new friend who, bored with his life and the friends he'd had since kindergarten, would see me as a novelty and we'd start hanging out. We'd generally do the basic Long Island things — smoke in the woods, walk to the record store and look at albums, eat crappy fast food — and just basically pal around consistently.

A month or two would go by in this blissful fashion, and then a combination of events would lead to my ouster and inevitable isolation. Generally, I'd do a "Billy" thing — this would most likely involve some kind of subtle disloyalty involving a girl my new friend and I both liked — and the friendship would begin to degrade. The guy's friends since birth whom he'd stopped hanging with would reappear and make a case for reinstatement, and this would finish the whole business.

Before I knew it, I'd be friendless and kind of floating around in this lonely limbo without anyone to talk to — or worse yet, I'd spend weeks and sometimes even months with the threat of someone being "after" me, and I'd live through the reality of getting beat up hundreds of times in my head before any real violence ever took place. My only comfort usually came from the fact that I knew that in nine more months we'd most likely be moving again.

By the time I was going into eighth grade, I was on my eighth move. Tired of the same old routine playing out over and over again, I began inventing elaborate lies that I started telling as soon as I met the kids in my new town. It's probably not much of a coincidence that this began right around the time girls became very important to me. Needless to say, they were terribly constructed stories, and I'd generally get busted in a matter of weeks. This led to further alienation.

This lifestyle I lived as a child did a few things to me. It ingrained in me the solid belief that life was always going to be a messy drama, but it was okay because there were always other towns, other people, and other schools. It also made me very hesitant to trust or love anyone, and this, in turn, informed my relationships later on with the opposite sex.

I graduated from high school in 1988 and went directly to a private college on Long Island that felt quite a bit like high school, part two. I mean, yes, we could smoke cigarettes in the cafeteria, but once that excitement wore off, it was more of the same pining away for girls I couldn't have and fragmented friendships with my peers. Don't forget to throw in a liberal number of platonic girlfriends; I practically owned property in the "friend zone."

In 1990, I applied and was accepted to the State University of New York at New Paltz, which was almost four hours from home. Leaving Long Island was a huge deal. I was excited about the prospect of being far from my parents, but I had no idea what I was about to encounter. Up until the day I arrived in New Paltz to begin my junior year, I was under the unconscious impression that the entire world acted like the people who lived on Long Island. The friend-zoning by girls — plus my issues with other guys — made me a very angry kid. Everything was always "fuck the world" and "the world sucks" when more appropriately it should have been "fuck Long Island" and "Long Island sucks."

I'm kidding. Sort of.

Whatever the case may be, I began meeting different, more interesting and artistic and less judgmental people. It felt so good that I never left. I still live here in New Paltz. It doesn't hurt that the Hudson Valley is a gorgeous part of the country. Having never been off Long Island for my first twenty years of life (with the exception of annual family vacations to Florida), I had never seen a mountain. If you've never seen upstate New York in autumn, you should. The sight of Mohonk and Minnewaska mountains, with their leaves turning gold and crimson and all varieties of burnt umber — it's spectacular. The first time I experienced it I understood what the word *majestic* truly meant. It filled my heart with awe and appreciation for Earth.

You would think this upgrade in environment and people would have resulted in me living happily ever after, but that was not to be — at least not for about twenty years. It took only a few days at my new college to kick off nearly two decades of substance abuse.

It started when everyone from my dorm suite got together with a neighboring suite to smoke a joint on move-in day — before classes even began. As I sat there and took my turn with the joint, the same old Billy record was playing in my mind, the one that said, "You are ugly. Girls really aren't that into you. You're probably going to be alone until you die." Obviously, these brain messages were instilled by a combination of being just twenty years old and my fabulous upbringing.

After we smoked the joint, we all decided to take a walk by what was commonly referred to as "the tripping fields." For the first time, I was stoned without being scared and completely paranoid. The trees and the wildflowers looked beautiful; as a matter of fact, I believe it was the first time I ever noticed how gorgeous the world was. Or how incredible cicadas sounded in the summer sun. Or how delicious ice-cold water tasted. Suddenly I realized that the Billy record — which played incessantly in my head every hour of every day — had stopped. Right then and there I made the resolution that I would never go another day on this planet without smoking pot. It was as if I had found my missing piece.

As I sat there on the grass, some of the other kids were playing Frisbee while others play-wrestled, guys and girls flirted, and this artsy girl off in the distance was working on something in her sketchbook. It was not as if I had never seen this sort of thing before, but it was the first time I observed things without a cynical and hurtful commentary playing in my brain. I was just a casual observer, and the only thing my brain was saying to me was that everything was going to be fine. I was going to meet someone beautiful and fall in love and enjoy life.

Sadly, my brain had immediately cemented an association

between everything being okay and being high. I had gotten stoned a couple times before when I lived on Long Island, but the combination of being free from my past and being free from my parents made everything very different.

Yup, I thought, *I definitely have to do this every day.*

Seven years later, I was in line at the Ulster County Methadone Clinic, my live-in girlfriend had been kidnapped and violently raped by our heroin dealer, and I was trying to figure out how much of "this and that" I'd have to take to go to sleep and never wake up again.

And you know, as horrible as that situation sounds, the fact that I made it through alive sometimes seemed worse. It was like living in a nightmare of prolonged agony that never ended. I knew I needed to stop using, and I could not stop. I went right on abusing substances and living an empty, sad life for thirteen years after all of that. There were hospitalizations, colon resections, dental abscesses, and overdoses. It just kept going on and on.

In addition to that, there were also all the embarrassing and awkward social situations I got into just as a matter of course. It got to the point where I'd walk down the street and get dirty looks or threats and have no idea what I'd done to provoke any of it. It felt like I spent more time in a walking blackout than in any other kind of state.

If you've been through this, and I'll assume you have or you wouldn't be reading this book, then you are aware of the emotions involved in trying to navigate through life with this cement monkey on your back. There are those few seconds every morning when you open your eyes and do the inventory: *Do I have any shit? How long is it going to last? When do I need to get more? How am I going to get it?*

And you know as well as I do that even on those super-rare

days when you have enough drugs to not have to be concerned with those things, it just clears the way to bug out about all the other things you've ignored while you were in survival mode. Things like, *When was the last time I paid rent?* Or even, *How did I get to this desperate and ugly place?* That particular one was my favorite.

As a matter of fact, almost every time I was able to feed the jones and not have to worry about the physical longings involved with the addiction, I always went straight to the place where I'd hate myself for becoming who I was. I knew in my heart that I was so much better than a rat chasing cheese every day.

Whether you can relate to this story or not, I am going to assume that you will agree with me that, yes, feelings are what led us to that drink, that pill, that hookup, that piece of cake, or that porn website. Let's be honest. Feelings have started wars. Feelings lead to people killing other people and forfeiting their freedom for decades behind bars. Feelings cause people to kill themselves in awful ways.

The bitch of the whole thing is that whatever you ingest to numb those feelings stops working very quickly, and all you are left with is the nonsensical compulsion to continue habits that are trying to kill you. (Actually, there's no proof that *porn* will kill you, but it can definitely lead to a sort of desensitization and/or erectile dysfunction, rendering most men wholly unable to carry on a loving and intimate relationship with a three-dimensional person, and who the hell wants to live without that, anyway?)

Now It's Your Turn:
Why Were You Getting High in the First Place?

I just bored you with the topsy-turvy story of my childhood because I was truly hoping to jump-start your memories. Can you remember the things along the way that paralyzed you and made it seem like a good idea to not feel anything, ever?

There's a fairly common trope in recovery that we all learn: *Using starts off as fun. Then it becomes fun with problems. And then it just becomes problems.* Think about what it was that led you to the dealer when it was just fun. And then think about what led you there again when it was fun with problems.

There is something inside you — some kind of pain, or emptiness, or both — that you were trying to fill. As a matter of fact, I'd venture to guess that even now that you are clean and sober, it still exists sometimes. Maybe even especially when life gets too crazy and you don't make it to enough meetings, or when old shit starts to kick up.

Ask yourself right here and right now what it is in your past that may manifest today as a need to log onto a porn site, or to chase a guy or a girl who you know is not right for you, or even to eat ridiculous amounts of chocolate or candy.

What hurt you enough to make you try to kill yourself with booze or dope or pills? What disconnected you from the rest of the universe? What story did your parents tell you and what story did you tell yourself that made you too scared to outwardly kill yourself — but half-assedly try to do it with the installment plan?

It's important to get in touch with this kind of stuff, because it helps to remember the mindset that led you down the path to nowhere. Did your parents completely misread you? Did they consider you a failure or a fuckup or a black sheep or a good-for-nothing? Did you, in turn, adopt their misguided theories about you? Or did society convince you that you weren't worth anything? Or maybe your parents tried their best, but the kids at school tortured you to a point where you saw yourself as a hopeless case.

To help you tap into those answers, try to picture yourself during your days of your most outlandish using. If someone very calmly tapped you on the shoulder at that point and asked, "Why are you doing what you're doing?" what might your answer have been? Was your plan to drink until you were dead? Were you just trying to get through that day? Did you have any kind of a plan at all? Whatever your answer may be, how did that attitude make you feel in your quiet moments when you couldn't lie to yourself anymore?

I learned to face these things as I attended meetings and worked the 12 steps with my sponsor. If you have any clean time, which, once again, I am assuming you do or you wouldn't be reading this book, then you've done the same. If for some reason you haven't gotten through at least the first four steps, I strongly suggest that you do. Once you realize what kinds of hidden resentments you've been carrying around for decades, you will begin to feel a sense of freedom that always eluded you while you were using.

Also, get yourself a piece of paper — or better still, a marble composition notebook — and do a couple of real short, painless writing exercises to help you get primed for your great transformation into rockstarhood. Ready? Here we go:

1. **Write down five things to congratulate yourself for.** I gave you a few ideas at the beginning of this chapter, but it really helps to write these things out and see them as belonging to you — not some stranger who wrote this book. What are five things you have accomplished that make you feel good about being you? And if you don't feel good about being you at this moment, what are five things you *should* be feeling good about? Remember, as long

as you're alive, you're still in the game. (There, I've given you something else to congratulate yourself for: you're alive!)

2. **Write three things that look completely different to you.** You know how when you first got clean you were thinking, *This is going to totally suck*, but then one night you found yourself at a table in a diner with some of the most loving people you've ever met? What experiences have you had that completely reframed how you thought life was going to be once you got clean? Write down three of these experiences. This will help you start to see how your thoughts, not your circumstances, control your life — because if you've had three experiences that surprised you by how much better they were than what you imagined, just think how many more surprising good developments are waiting for you.

As you join me on this journey to find the greatest self you can become, I need you to know this: there will be challenges. The very things that have haunted you in the past will inevitably crop back up along the way. By taking the time now to look back and objectively name which kinds of circumstances and thoughts triggered you in the past, you'll better prepare yourself to stay steady when shit happens in the future.

This process is very much like birth and usually just as painful, but in the same way you used your grit, your desire, and your strength to turn one day clean into two days clean, you can use them to transform your life. One foot in front of the other. One challenge at a time. Until your craziest dreams are becoming reality.

When you were using, the idea of getting a year clean almost seemed impossible, didn't it? But look, either you've gone and done it or you're well on your way. It's the same with becoming a madly successful achievement machine. After all, you've already done the impossible. Everything that follows from now on will be pretty easy compared with what detox was like. Believe that you can do it.

CHAPTER TWO

Name Your *Why*

What we learn at meetings is that we often have to hit a brick wall at full speed numerous times before we achieve what is known as the *gift of desperation*. Desperation isn't that fun, but it's a gift because it makes you realize what you are desperate for — what you want more than anything else. Once you are crystal clear on that information, you can use it to motivate yourself to go about the sometimes-tedious work to get a day, a week, a month, or a year clean. You need to have a desire to break free from your addiction that is *almost* bigger than your desire to be alive. The same is true for the fabulous life that awaits you — you have to jones for having more money than you need, work that you care about and that contributes to society, and solid relationships with people who love you and see the best in you.

Remember the first time you fell in love in junior high school? Do you remember how badly you wanted to be with that person and how you thought about them day and night? You need to long for the life of your dreams more than that. Remember how bad you wanted to be a grown-up when you were fourteen years old? More than that. It requires a level of desire that is practically unmatched by anything you've ever wanted before — except, of course, for whatever it is you're in recovery from. You've already got well-developed "wanting" muscles; now it's time to put them to use desiring things that make your life better, not worse.

What the 12-step programs call the "gift of desperation" I call the "gift of definiteness of purpose." Definiteness of purpose is exactly the tool I used to raise myself from a cab driver earning $350 per week to a truck driver earning $1,000 per week in a matter of months. While I will elucidate what I did to get there, keep in mind that I had absolutely no aptitude for or experience in truck driving. In fact, when I was in truck-driving school, the prospect of driving that truck with the instructor sitting next to me gave me an acidy stomachache and made me feel like I needed to use the bathroom. And the very idea of having to someday drive that thing with *no one* sitting next to me gave me nightmares. It was the most unnatural and scary thing I have ever done — and consider that I did a lot of crazy shit when I was using, such as driving around with an ounce of coke on me or copping on a heavily patrolled block in the Bronx.

What is so ironic about the whole situation is that there were ten other guys and girls in my class, all of whom were much more comfortable with tractor trailers, and not a single one of them is gainfully employed in this profession today.

The difference was that my eyes were fixed firmly on the prize. I had "definiteness of purpose." And I had it because I had a rock-solid reason *why* I wanted and needed this career change: my girlfriend was pregnant. As a result, what I wanted more than anything in the world was to be a breadwinner. I had already experienced the heartbreak of being estranged from a child (my oldest daughter, from an earlier relationship) because of my decades-long struggle with substance abuse. This was my last chance to be a clean dad who was present in my child's life. *Not* landing a job that more than doubled my salary simply wasn't an option. I became a person of indomitable spirit.

I don't know you yet, and I don't know what you have going on in your brain or what your IQ is, but the incredible part is that it doesn't matter the least little bit. You don't have to be a brainiac to be a person of indomitable spirit who has definiteness of purpose. In case you haven't figured it out by now, I'm no Albert Einstein. And that's totally fine, because what drives all of us in this world is not intelligence but *emotion*. If you can summon a strong enough emotion about a particular goal, you can absolutely accomplish it. For me, that emotion was the kick in the gut I felt whenever I thought of that beautiful little girl whom I never had the chance to kiss good night or tuck into bed because of my using. When I realized that someone else might end up doing that in my place with this new baby who was on the way, it built a strong enough *why* in me to virtually move mountains — or drive a vehicle that I could swear was the size of a small mountain.

Human beings are emotionally and psychologically complicated, but our motivations are quite simple. We run entirely on the principle of pain and pleasure. If you think about what made you drink or drug or overeat, it boiled down to the fact that it made you feel better — even if it was just for the moment. And you got into recovery the moment that the pain of whatever you were doing outweighed the dread of the thought of stopping.

What I would suggest you do if you'd like to begin *your* transformation is get out a notebook. If you don't have one, buy one. I'm serious — a little black-and-white marble composition notebook that you can buy for two dollars. Someday, when your life is totally different, you'll find that notebook, and you'll be able to lose yourself in giddy gratitude that you did this little exercise and began the process of changing the trajectory of your entire life.

Once you have your notebook, open it up, and at the top of the first blank page, write the word *Why*. Now, here's the tricky part: the pain you feel about everything you are missing out on due to earning *just enough* money every week to get by — you know, the pain you spend an awful lot of energy trying *not* to think about — is what I want you to think about. It could be having to tell your kids that "someday" you will all go on vacation — knowing full well it's highly unlikely that someday will ever come. It could be having to ask your neighbor for a ride to work because your rickety car keeps breaking down any time the temperature dips below forty degrees. Or more serious stuff, like not being able to help your mom or dad when they're in a jam. Reacquaint yourself intimately with whatever causes you the most pain about your current situation, and write it all down.

On the next page in your book, write *My Future* and, below that, describe how you see your life once you have found a way to earn twice or three times as much as you are earning now. Pick a nice round number like $1,000 per week. Let me give you some advice: you're not going to be able to work yourself into the kind of emotional frenzy you'll need to be in to make this happen by writing "It'll be really cool." Describe, in exacting detail, what a normal day will be like for you once you have access to that kind of money every week.

As you are writing all this down, keep in mind that this is not some ridiculous fantasy I am trying to sell you. I was where you are, and now I am taking that money home every week. You have every reason in the world to believe that it's available to you, too. All you need to do is make two hard-core decisions. First, that you want to earn this money, and second, that you will stick with it if it begins to get tough.

The reason I asked you to write those two pages in your new journal is because you are going to need an incredible amount of desire. Remember, I said it was available to you; I never said it was going to be a breeze. If it was, everyone would be taking home $1,000 per week. I look around at the people I work with every day — all of us making that much — and I can promise you: there's nothing they possess physically or mentally that you don't. In fact, I'd be willing to bet that no matter who you are, you won't have as tough a time as I did.

When I finished truck-driving school, I still didn't really know how to drive a truck, but I was lucky enough to get a job where they provided an extensive six-week training period. So, picture it: living in a truck with your teacher for a month and a half. In my case, my teacher — or mentor, as they were called — had no easy time of it. I'm a musician and a writer and just really the kind of guy who shouldn't be around power tools or large vehicles. It was not a match made in heaven, but this poor trainer tried as hard as he could to get me ready to go out and do the job on my own.

As time went on, I got the hang of everything — except backing up. Now, I wasn't aware of this when I first had the idea to learn this profession, but you simply cannot do this job if you do not become an expert at backing up. Think about it: I would be delivering stuff to people in stores. They'd be waiting for their stuff in the loading dock. There's only one way to get a truck into a loading dock — backing up. Getting the stuff in my truck to the people in the store is the main reason for this job.

And I just could not do it right. The third week came and went. Then the fourth. And there I was — the trailer going too far to the right, too far to the left, almost hitting everything in sight and giving my mentor a serious case of agita. It got to the point of feeling hopeless. Somehow, though, when I thought about what was at stake, I kept right on trying, the same way I would have if my dealer kept letting my call go to voicemail. I was becoming someone with an *indomitable spirit*.

I'd love to be able to tell you that by the time the six weeks were up, I was a pro at backing into loading docks — but I gave up lying soon after I got clean. I was horrible. I did, however, have a few things on my side. First, my pit-bull tenacity that drove me to keep trying no matter what; and second (and probably more important), the substantial driver shortage — that is, by the way, still going on — in the trucking industry.

Either way, I made it happen, and I can't help feeling and believing in my heart that if I could work my way up the ranks in a profession I truly had no business being involved in, you can, too! Whoever you are and whatever it is you are trying to do. Whether your name is Kevin or Kaitlyn. The only thing that truly matters is that you have a strong enough *why*.

So, review what you wrote down in your notebook just now. Does the first page create enough pain for you to feel compelled to make a big change? If it doesn't, keep writing. I know it might feel shitty to commit to paper the very things you've spent so much time, energy, and brain cells avoiding. But the truth is, if you don't get honest with yourself about what's at stake, your life is not likely to change.

Does the second page you wrote — the one where you

imagined the things you'd have and do with twice as much money coming in every week — transform you into an overly excited maniac ready to conquer the world? If not, go back and spice that up a little bit.

Clearly, because you picked up this book, you are ready for something better. I know you've done way scarier things in your life in the name of feeling how you want to feel, so put that pit-bull tenacity and single-minded focus to use here to get crystal clear on your *why*. It's your golden ticket to the chocolate factory.

Creating a Life on *Your* Terms

In the 12-step programs, we are taught to accept life as it is. People in the meetings often refer to this as "life on life's terms." But I beg to differ.

During my first couple of years of meetings, I came to see the "life on life's terms" label being applied to all kinds of realities that were just not necessary — like trying to make ends meet while working at Walmart and eating Top Ramen every night. That is not life on life's terms. That's a fucking drag.

The first trucking company that hired me bused me out to their terminal in the next state and, upon seeing my skills (or lack of skills), promptly fired me and sent me back home three days later. Waiting eight hours in Grand Central station for my connecting bus to take me back home to my nervous and pregnant girlfriend — that, my friends, was *life on life's terms.*

Just as with any other deal, you don't have to accept the terms. When you know there's something better available — and you are perfectly clear on why you want and need something better — you'll find that you can push against that resistance and it will yield.

The idea behind the third step in a 12-step program is that

you have *to first* put massive legwork into the creation of a better life, *and then* leave the results up to God.

When I made the decision to turn my will and my life over to the care of God as I understood Him, I did not make some agreement to keep driving a cab until God gave me something better and more profitable to do.

Don't get me wrong. I love 12-step programs. As a matter of fact, I do not think it would have been possible for me to get to where I am today, sitting in my little hideaway in New Paltz and writing this book, without the daily support of my sponsor and my dear friends in the program. I have a network of support that not many people possess, and for this, I am eternally grateful. My point is that there is a lot of oral tradition in 12-step programs, and with oral tradition, there are many different and personal translations.

I have never believed that God's will is for us to try to survive in a constant state of lack. I believe that we are to strive for abundance so that we may have the ability to give freely of our resources and our time to those less fortunate than ourselves. I mean, doesn't that seem more Godlike than living in poverty?

My undying determination to learn how to drive a massive truck — that ability inside me to face the stomach-churning fear of getting outside my comfort zone and getting good at what I was never really meant to be good at — was the same thing that had propelled me from my first terrible day clean to my one-year anniversary of recovery. You've got it, too. It should be spelled out right there in your trusty marble composition notebook (you did go and get one, didn't you?).

Let's review the takeaways: on the first page of your notebook, you wrote down everything that makes you sad or upset about living in a constant state of lack, of trying to run your life on a $400 paycheck, of being on a first-name basis with

Daphne from the collection agency. On the next page in your notebook, you painted a clear picture of what your life will be like once you are happily getting that $1,000 paycheck every week. This is your *why*.

These next six items will be your *how*. Some of it you will do in your notebook, and some of it is a little arts-and-crafty, but stay with me anyway. This is how it all begins. Like I said, get excited. Life is about to take a very significant turn for you.

1. Up Your Value

What will you be contributing to the world that will qualify you for the abundance you are seeking to acquire in your life? Here's what I mean: When I was a rural taxi driver earning $350 a week, I was shuffling people who were also earning $350 a week to and from work. Useful, yes, but only to a point. When I learned to drive a rig, I was able to transport tons of merchandise — and value — from here to there in a matter of hours. This was way more useful, and because of that, the universe was bestowing upon me three times more money every week. Once it became clear to me that the universe delivered value in accordance with how much value I produced, I began to exchange more beneficial services for even greater rewards.

You can also expand on this over time, just like I did. Once I had a bunch more money to work with, I was able to go to a recording studio and make some really well-produced recordings of my music. This, in turn, led to paying gigs at various venues near where I live. Just as a matter of course, my gigs at these few places led to even more venues, and this all turned into a lucrative side hustle for me. Any kind of side hustle is a good thing, but can you imagine having one where you get to do what you love? That's nothing short of a blessing.

On the third page of your notebook, let your brain run

wild. Write the heading *Ways to Up My Value*, and jot down any and all talent you have that you could develop into your own side hustle to make a few hundred extra dollars every week. Let me give you an example: When I did this exercise, one thing I wrote down was "Book paying gigs at local venues." It initially seemed crazy to think anyone would pay me to do that because in the past, I'd get booked here and there and the pay was always spotty — but after I wrote it down, I began to brainstorm a way to level up to professional caliber. It didn't turn out exactly as I wrote it on paper, but just putting the idea down in a notebook was enough to begin to bring it into reality.

2. Name Your Sacrifice

I am, of course, not sure about your personal situation, but one thing I am certain of is that whatever it is, it's going to change drastically when you make the decision to go for it. I don't want to give you a boring lesson on word derivation, but I think it's important to realize that the word *decision* is very close to the word *incision*. You are figuratively cutting away all other possibilities except for the one goal that you have set for yourself.

I am sure by now you've gotten the gist of my story. I practically broke up with my comfort zone to get into the world of truck driving. I lived in the back of that truck, and I endured the pain of seeing my daughter's first steps and first words on Facebook rather than in person. It was no day at the beach, but in retrospect, I'd do it all over again if I had to.

On the fourth page of your notebook, put the word *Sacrifice* and write out what you'd be willing to face for the chance to change everything about your life. Would you study day and night to get your Registered Nurse credential? Would you go to school for a couple of years to become a surgical technologist?

Would you spend a year sleeping in the back of a Kenworth and drive all over the country?

These are all important things to consider, and when you write out this page, try to get real quiet and listen to your inner voice. No one is suggesting that you have to be gung ho about throwing yourself into a lower quality of life for all eternity, but if you are looking to really improve things for yourself, you should get comfortable with the fact that you're probably going to spend a little time being really *un*comfortable.

3. *Do One Thing* Right Now to Move Toward That Goal

Notice that I said "do" — that does not mean plan to google commercial driving schools tomorrow. It means call right now and ask them to mail you a catalog. It means drive to the community college in your town and get a continuing-education brochure *today*. You can take the next step tomorrow. And then the next, and the next after that. Just never get stuck in the idea that you have to wait before you do anything. There is always some step that's available to you *right now*.

After you've made this step, take out your notebook and work on the fifth page. Title it *Action I Took*, and describe, in detail, the single step that you made toward your new goal. Go on and write about how much pleasure you felt from following through and getting the ball in motion. Did it fill you with a new sense of self-confidence you hadn't felt in a while? Is this a feeling that you could, perhaps, get used to?

As you may have figured out already, there are some definite similarities between what we are doing here — when we seize the day and take action — and that moment when we found ourselves seeking out our new lives in recovery. For me, there was that same sense of relief and hope that things were sure to start getting better. Of course, I am once again bringing up the pleasure/pain principle, but only because it works so well. Human beings love to feel pleasure and avoid pain at all costs. Writing page five will help you to keep associating your movement toward your goal with the incredible feeling that progress gives you.

4. Stay Present to Your Goals

Every single morning — seven days a week — pull out that notebook and read what you wrote during the exercises in this chapter. I am not suggesting this because it's good luck. I am telling you to do this because it will begin to activate a process in your brain that is referred to as the *reticular activating system* (RAS), which is a fancy way of saying that your brain will become like a heat-seeking missile, drawing to you exactly what you want or need. The RAS is responsible for that strange phenomenon that happens when you buy a new blue Honda Civic and then start seeing them everywhere. They were always everywhere — you just didn't "see" them.

Our brains are incredibly complex, but just as you don't need to be able to understand the intricacies of programming and code to log onto Instagram, or the scientific principles of electricity to turn on the bathroom light, you don't need to know brain science to use the gift of RAS to your advantage. There is so much stimulation going on around you that if you paid attention to all of it, you'd probably go mad in about five minutes. Because of this, your brain expends as much energy figuring out what *not* to pay attention to as it does on what to pay attention to.

When you read those few pages every morning, your brain will subconsciously be on the lookout for opportunities to move closer to what you need in order to make your dreams come true. You'll notice the right people just showing up to help you and the right circumstances appearing out of nowhere. This isn't hocus-pocus; it's just the way our brains work.

Read them! Every. Single. Morning.

5. Make a Vision Board

A vision board is a bulletin board, or a piece of posterboard or even cardboard, that you fill with images that represent your biggest dreams and aspirations. These boards found their way into popular culture from that movie *The Secret,* but don't let that scare you. Pop icon Beyoncé, talk-show host Ellen DeGeneres, and life coaches from coast to coast have extolled the virtues of vision boards for years. When you possess visual representations of everything you want from life, you are once again kicking your reticular activating system into gear. It essentially trains your brain to look for golden opportunities the way a good running back knows how to find the hole.

I remember hearing the story of Lisa Erspamer. In high school in the late eighties, she was given an assignment to make a vision board. She was always interested in working in television, so she glued a photo of Oprah on her board and wrote "Executive Producer" underneath it. On January 1, 2011, Erspamer began her position as the executive producer of *The Oprah Winfrey Show.* There are many other such stories, but suffice it to say, a vision board is an effective tool.

I would assume the reason there are so many naysayers when it comes to utilizing these kinds of things is because — well, there are naysayers about everything. If you took my life story, for instance, and asked a run-of-the-mill negative person if it seemed possible, I am pretty sure their answer would be, "No...there is no way a junkie could possibly get clean, learn a lucrative profession, write articles that thousands of people read and enjoy, and then go on to write a book." And yet, here you are reading that very book by that very guy. My point? Don't believe the hype. Anything is possible.

Now go and get yourself about four magazines. Don't choose ones you'd typically read. Expand your horizons. If you're the kind of guy or girl who digs motocross, get copies of *Cosmo* and *National Geographic*.

Next, go through those magazines and cut out photos, words, and images that represent your dreams, and glue, tape, or tack them onto your board, as a collage. If you come across a picture of Costa Rica and your dream is to someday surf in Hawaii, don't let that be an issue. Cut it out and tell yourself it's Hawaii. Symbolism works fine. Cut out a photo of the car you see yourself driving and the house you want. The sky's the limit.

It never hurts to suspend disbelief and really go for it. In other words, no one has ever regretted having a positive outlook and setting goals for themselves. I can promise you that the same cannot be said for negative people who were too afraid to try to do anything besides exist from one day to the next. You get one life. This is not a dress rehearsal.

6. Buckle Up...

Because your life is about to change!

CHAPTER THREE

Change Your Thoughts, Change Your Life

When you can see how your life story has been teaching you exactly what you need in order to be able to create and maintain the life you want, it changes everything. You stop seeing problems and start seeing possibilities. This is when things really start heating up, because when you change your thoughts, my friend, you absolutely change your life.

What's been keeping you from having a positive outlook and being hopeful about the future isn't your circumstances, your personality, or your genetic makeup. Nope — it's your thoughts. You probably don't realize it, but you have thinking habits that you've carried around since childhood. These old thoughts may feel as comfortable and cozy as the blankie you used to insist on sleeping with every night, but they aren't. They are actually the source of all the discomfort and pain in your life. It's time to expose these thoughts for what they really are — destructive falsehoods.

Let me tell you about an incident that happened with me — yes, me with my multiple years clean — that may shed some light on this. I was driving with my six-year-old and three-year-old daughters in the car when the guy in the truck behind us began to tailgate us very dangerously. I was already going forty-five miles per hour in a thirty zone, but I almost think he wanted me to go sixty or sixty-five. It was total insanity. When I pulled over to let him by, he got out of his truck and came over, trying to get into an altercation. As I said, my daughters were strapped in their car seats in the back. I had to back down. It was the only responsible thing to do. Besides, truth be told, he was about a hundred pounds heavier and a foot taller than I am.

This was just the sort of thing that, at one time in my life, would have made me want to use or drink. I felt humbled and spineless in front of my children, and my old way would have been to ruminate on those feelings until getting fucked up was the only thing that made any sense.

Most of what sets us off is usually the direct result of the faulty wiring we developed in childhood. In a case like this, my daughters weren't disappointed in me for not getting out to fight the guy. The way I handled it most likely saved them from having to experience a traumatic episode that would have stayed with them forever — things I would not have realized during my using days. So, you can see how important it can be to rewire your mind and change the way you perceive reality.

Bear with me, this is slippery stuff, but it is absolutely essential that you get your head wrapped around it. Mastering this process will not only be super helpful — I promise that it will change your entire quality of life.

Your Power to Decide

It says in the Basic Text of Narcotics Anonymous — and it has been proved over time to be true in every case — that judges, probation officers, and therapists can never force anyone to get clean. Everyone who has ever gotten clean has done it because *they* themselves decided it was time. And that decision generally comes after you've reached the mythical crossroads where you realize you have a basic choice: quit using or die.

This holds true even for what are known as "high-bottom addicts" — meaning addicts who still had a job, a house, a car, and a marriage by the time they reached the crossroads. It's just that "death" for them was not quite as dramatic as a flatline on a heart-rate monitor. It may have been that they woke up one morning, looked in the mirror, and realized that they had become the complete antithesis of everything they imagined for themselves as children, or that they experienced a cavernous feeling in their chest where they realized their life had lost all meaning.

I walked around for an entire decade anchored to a methadone bottle for fear of what it was going to feel like when I tried to get off it. Now, it certainly wasn't a lot of methadone. As a matter of fact, I got through the entire week on someone else's "daily" dose, but the quantity isn't the point. The point is that for ten years I could not do anything or go anywhere — whether that was to travel or to move to a new apartment — because that orange albatross was around my neck. Anytime I had to endure an entire *day* without it, it seemed like torture. My legs would get charley horses, my eyes would water, my nose would run, and I didn't have enough energy to get up off the couch. And I knew from everything I had read and everyone in my circle that it took six weeks to get through withdrawal, and it would get worse and worse every day that I was away from it.

My enduring fantasy of how I was going to get clean and live happily ever after was that I'd get in a car wreck, fall into a coma, and wake up six weeks later completely detoxed. I am embarrassed to say that that really was my "plan." Unfortunately, when two years became five and then became ten, I started to face the possibility that the coma strategy might not work.

As the years went on, my body had a harder and harder time tolerating the amount of drugs that my brain seemed to need. My torso was distended, and I looked awful because I hardly ever had a bowel movement. I got so uncomfortable that I went to a doctor, who took one look at me and insisted I go for a colonoscopy.

When I woke up from the colonoscopy the doctor said — far too cheerily, I might add — that I wasn't going anywhere.

"That colon has to come out! That thing is finished," he chirped.

My head was still swimming from the anesthesia, and I wasn't sure I completely understood. After the doctor and his entourage of students meandered out of the room while gossiping about whoever had been on *American Idol* the night before and how one of them was simply dying for a yogurt, the attending nurse explained to me that I was going in for surgery in the morning and the doctor would be removing my large intestine.

"How am I going to live without a large intestine?" I whimpered.

"Well, the doctor will install what is known as an ostomy, and you will have a bag that you go to the bathroom in," she explained as she rubbed my shoulder in her "be a big boy now" fashion.

When she left the room, I lay there with tears streaming down my cheeks as I tried to face the reality of being a thirty-three-year-old with a huge ego and no self-esteem shitting rather publicly into a colostomy bag for the rest of my life. I resolutely decided then and there that that was not for me. I'd let them do what they were going to do and then jump off the bridge in Rosendale, New York — the closest bridge I knew of that was high enough to kill me.

When I woke up the next day in the intensive care unit, I felt around at my torso looking for my new poop receptacle. The ICU nurse came to check on me, and I asked about "the bag."

"What bag?" she asked.

"The colostomy bag."

"Oh, I think you're confused. You don't have a colostomy bag," she assured me.

I wasn't sure what any of it meant, but I remember passing back out in a state of inexplicable relief. I might be dreaming, I thought, but it was a pretty nice dream.

I learned later that I had been blessed to get a young surgeon who was visiting from Italy and knew how to do what was considered to be a very artistic resection of my bowel. He saved me from having to live with a colostomy bag for the rest of my life. You'd think that after this type of miracle I would thank God for sparing me, turn over a new leaf, and start going from town to town extolling the virtues of a clean life and surgeons from Italy, right?

Nope. I had been home from the hospital for two days before I got into my beat-up Geo Metro and drove from Port Jervis to New Paltz to get the bottle of methadone that I desperately needed to wash down the Percocet they had given me for my surgical recovery. That wouldn't have been so terrible except that I had to drive with one foot on the gas and one on the brake to keep from stalling (I told you that my Geo Metro was beat-up — it barely ran), and the two hours of doing that really bothered the metal staples that were holding my guts together.

Nope, not ready to change yet.

What finally did get me to change was, no surprise, heartbreak. At the time of my surgery, the mother of my first child and I had been separated for a year and a half already. I had been so wrapped up in my self-centeredness that I had been in denial about the end of that relationship, thinking that surely we would get back together any day. So when she called me right before Independence Day in 2005 and told me she had met a new guy at an NA meeting, I felt the world come crashing down around me. The pain of the very real possibility that my four-year-old daughter was going to be growing up in a house with another man as her male parent made me want to die.

I texted her that there was no reason for me to live anymore, and instead of consoling me, she presented me with the full fury of her newly indoctrinated recovery-speak and told me to stop feeling sorry for myself, get off my pathetic ass, and go to a meeting. That made me so angry. I remember devising a plan (I always made great plans in those days) that I would go to a meeting, get clean, and then meet someone. I'd show her!

I wasn't motivated by the best of intentions, but that moment is when I decided to get clean.

I did, too. Even though this all happened in 2005, I remember that six-week period of kicking methadone like it was last month. The term *restless leg syndrome* does not even scratch the surface. I wanted to chop my legs off. I also did not sleep for three and a half weeks.

I realize that a lot of people bandy around the phrase *I did not sleep* as a way to describe a tough night — but make no mistake about what I am telling you: I *did not sleep* for three and a half weeks. At times I ingested twenty-five or more Benadryl pills and I would still be wide awake for the entire night. Even though my body felt like it had a four-hundred-pound bowling ball resting on top of it, I still didn't sleep. I would spend the whole night lumbering down the stairs, hoisting myself into the hot tub that came with my apartment and filled up with orangey-brown water that the landlord swore to me was only rust, and then trying to haul my heavy-as-shit body back up to bed before the leg pains would return. It never worked. I'd be out of that orange toxic soup for less than five minutes, and those charley horses would come back worse than before — kind of like they were pissed that I was trying to get rid of them.

I started this deplorable process on July 4. I drove an hour to attend my first meeting, and it had a profound effect on me. I didn't see anyone there I wanted to date, but I *did* hear the message, and it was powerful enough to fill me with hope and a mission. The message was so compelling, in fact, that I went to a meeting every night of the entire six-week period of kicking.

I had been in isolation with my drug habit for so long that I almost gladly endured the abysmal pain of detoxing because the loving support network of new friends felt so incredibly good. For the first time in almost a dozen years I had people in my life who cared about me and talked to me even if I didn't have money or drugs. They held my hand and loved me — and actually still love me now, thirteen years later.

If you've been paying attention, you may remember that I said I've been clean for nine years, not thirteen. Relapse, as the cliché goes, is part of my story. We'll get to that later on. The point I am making is that the human brain is extraordinarily powerful. Sometimes when I share at a meeting that I spent the obligatory six weeks of physically detoxing off methadone working every day and going to meetings every night, people don't believe me. What these same people often fail to realize is that we, as human beings, are capable of almost unbelievable feats at times. That's how huge the power of decision is.

This can be a slippery area to discuss because die-hard 12-step people will insist that we never get clean by our own will, and that it is *God's* will we need to be grateful for. I believe this to be a misinterpretation. Yes, when we turn our wills and our lives over to the care of God, we are well on our way to a better life. But it is our *decision* and our will that drive us to put down the poison and sit in that meeting chair. I like to see it as a collaborative effort.

Whether you buy into my view or not, you have to at least admit that the quality of your life is a direct result of the quality of your thoughts. I know this because I experienced an entire shift in my life from going to that first meeting. Nothing in my circumstances changed in the hour I was inside that church basement. Only my thoughts changed. I became way more grateful to be alive. I felt connected to people. I felt hopeful about my future. And it was all because I had decided to show up.

Yes, rent was still due on the first of the month. Yes, I still had to go to work on Monday morning. No matter how good the meeting was, that stuff never changed. What *did* change, however, was what I thought and how I felt about those things. I was happy to have an apartment and a job, because I was reminded, while in a meeting, that there are millions of people in the world who would give anything for those same circumstances.

You Have Already Decided to Change Your Life...
Now Use It for Even Greater Good

If you went through NA like me, think back to when you got your first thirty-day key tag. Do you remember what it felt like to hold that little orange tag and get that hug from your meeting leader? Do you remember getting so excited to stay clean for another thirty days so you could get the green key tag? C'mon, you know you got jazzed when you got a tangible form of recognition for your efforts.

It's not even remotely close to how you thought you'd feel when you stopped getting high, right? Didn't you expect your life to be really boring and uninspiring? But making progress feels *good*. It creates its own force field that can compel you to keep going, if you harness it. Sadly, I do not believe that 12-step programs do a good job of channeling the good feelings those early achievements create.

I am certain — and I say *certain* because I lived through this and I've watched many other people live through it, too — that after we get our first year clean, the excitement starts to die down. We don't get all that attention anymore, and milestones are a lot further apart. It almost seems as though we sort of fade into the background until we get through another year — *if* we get through another year. This is why I will always be convinced that we should use the momentum we've built up from the achievements of that first year clean and apply that hard-won mojo to our lives outside the meeting rooms of NA and AA. I mean, obviously we need the program as a foundation, but it's a really strong foundation — so strong that you can use it to build a fabulous life on top of it, complete with a new career in trucking. Or nursing. Or surgical technology. Or any trade where they desperately need us and are willing to fill our pockets with $1,000 a week as long as we take the time to jump through the hoops to learn exactly what it is they need from us. And that will be just the beginning.

I admit that, yes, for me there are days when I am so sick of driving a truck. But now I have a history of setting my sights on what was once the "impossible" and making it possible. I know that I am very close to hanging up the keys to that truck and starting a new career of writing and coaching, because I have real experience making things grow bigger and better, and it all began with my desire to earn that next key tag and receive that next hug.

Let's Rewire Your Thoughts

Really, the only thing that changed about me — between the time I was a sloth driving around in a twenty-year-old Geo Metro copping methadone and hoping to get in a near-fatal, coma-inducing collision and now, when I'm a guy who has thousands of people a month reading my articles and a book deal — is my thoughts.

Better circumstances will come only when your thoughts change. Even if by some stroke of luck your circumstances improved drastically before you did any work on improving your thoughts, it wouldn't last. Because you wouldn't have the capacity to appreciate your new situation. If you don't learn to have gratitude for the gift of waking up every morning — of having working legs and arms, of being alive — then you won't have gratitude for making more money than you need to survive.

So, let's do this:

1. **For each of the following hypothetical scenarios, write what could be a positive outcome.** (For example, if one scenario were "You broke

your toe," a positive outcome could be that you get a week off from work and, while you're laid up, inadvertently wind up reading a book that changes your life.)

    (a) Your lover breaks up with you.

    (b) You get fired from your job.

    (c) You get a flat tire on the way to work.

    (d) You drop your phone in the toilet.

2. **Think about a time when you did what you once thought was impossible.** It could be when you quit smoking cigarettes; left a crappy relationship; or, yes, walked into a recovery meeting and got your first day sober. Get clear on what was happening inside you when you made that decision. That very thing is what you need to draw on to change your thoughts, too — that inner voice that says, *That's it! No more! The end!* Once you have a clear picture of that moment — well, you know... take out your notebook. Write a few paragraphs about that day. Really get as descriptive as you possibly can. The better you're able to put this down on paper, the better your chances will be to jumpstart those "change" muscles again.

3. **On the next page, describe your gratitude for your ideal new life as if it has already happened.** This exercise of showing gratitude in advance of something, often called *affirmation*, has been used for centuries by people who visualize change — and it works so well, it's freaky.

When you're done with these steps, you'll have two or more pages that will essentially send a signal to the universe that you're ready to receive all that you're dreaming of. This is when shit starts to get real.

Once you have done these things, you have aligned yourself — in a very tangible way — with a new reality. You have set an intention, and once you set an intention, you are halfway home.

CHAPTER FOUR

Start Making $1,000 a Week

As I said in the previous chapter, once I cut alcohol and substances out of the picture, I was getting my thrills and my dopamine — the brain's feel-good chemical — first in the form of sobriety key tags and then eventually by the big one-year anniversary and cake that the 12-step program gave me. I don't want to paint an unrealistic picture of what my first year sober was like: obviously, we all know that it's never all peaches and cream. But that's exactly why the program was working so well for me. I was experiencing so many different emotional challenges that it became clear to me that I would not have had a chance to stay in recovery and not relapse without this new ragtag family around me. For me, like a lot of guys, among the biggest challenges was the celibacy clause.

As you may already know, one of the first suggestions that we hear when we walk into the rooms of NA and AA is to abandon any idea of getting involved with someone romantically for at least our first year. Most of the old-timers will tell you that, in their experience, a person's chances of success and subsequent survival are increased if they put a yearlong moratorium on dating and divert all those energies toward self-care and self-love. The explanation is that for many of us with various addictive tendencies, the habit is to put our focus on almost anything other than ourselves. When you think about it, even when nonaddicted people first fall in love, they put everything they have into the new relationship. This goes double for someone who just started a life in recovery.

It wasn't too difficult for me to follow this suggestion. As is typically the case, my girlfriend and I had broken up a few months before I officially hit bottom. When I made the decision to get sober, I left the apartment we shared, and I moved into an old widow's boardinghouse, 10 miles north, in Kingston. That was where the taxi company I worked for was, and there were meetings within walking distance seven days a week. More importantly, the old widow was serious about the "no guests in your room" policy and thought nothing of issuing an immediate eviction should you decide to ignore this. I spent my first six months of sobriety living like a hair-shirt ascetic.

After that period of abject poverty and celibacy, I called my ex-girlfriend and asked her if she'd sleep with me for my birthday, which was rapidly approaching. We'd managed to maintain a halfway decent friendship through texting, and she'd never struggled with social conventions or inhibitions, so she agreed. Everyone in my little support network warned me that this was a stupid idea, but I was convinced I knew better. It was not a new relationship. It was not a relationship at all. It was a night of passion — a release. It was something I really needed.

It was a stupid idea.

The next morning, my brain hurt. My ex drove me home

from the hotel where we'd spent the night, and I lumbered sadly back into my room. My emotions were all strange and low frequency. Something just wasn't right. I called in sick at the taxi company and just lay there in bed, staring at the box of condoms with one missing. I'm still not sure what it was, but it felt like loss. Like I was mourning something.

I remember going to a meeting that night and sharing about this. Everybody laughed. Not so much in an "I told you so" way, but in a "Who the hell calls in sick, lies in bed, and stares at an opened box of condoms?" way.

Regardless of this misstep, I was bound and determined to make recovery work this time around. This part of it was always super difficult for me. I love falling in love. I love being in love. I love relationships. I love sex. In fact, I've been told by friends throughout the years that this might have been a bigger issue for me than drugs. Fortunately, my higher power (or the universe, if you like) conspired to do for me what I was not able to do for myself.

It became clear to me after my birthday that I needed to stay as far away from my recent ex as I possibly could. So, when I wasn't engaged with thoughts of recovery like I should have been, I began to think about an ex-girlfriend from twenty years before. She and I had become reacquainted through Facebook while "condom ex" and I were still together, and I began to daydream about rekindling things with her. It came on slowly, but as I was approaching my first-year anniversary of sobriety, she was all I could think about.

To this day, I'm not sure if she just wasn't convinced that I was a good idea or if she cared about me enough to steer clear of me until my first-year celebration, but we managed to stay platonic until that time. A few days after my anniversary meeting, she and I went out to dinner in Woodstock — a town that breathes romance and musical history — and got caught in a late-summer downpour as we left the restaurant. Drenched and giddy in her Jeep, we turned to each other and kissed for the first time since the early nineties. It was a lot different this time, though. I fell madly in love with her.

That small window of time when I had just celebrated my first year, coupled with kissing this woman I'd had my sights set on for what felt like an eternity, was crazy good. I followed suit and did what I usually did — which was to put all my focus into this new romance. She and I reached a heightened level of intimacy with incredible speed, and before long we began to discuss starting a family.

I don't blame you if you think this sounds nuts. This is what addicts do, right? As crazy as it sounds, she had reached a chronological point where she felt it was time to have children, and I wanted a second chance at doing fatherhood right. We had known each other since we were both still hiding our cigarettes from our parents, and our pimples from each other, so it didn't seem so far-fetched.

What did seem far-fetched was my ability to swing it financially. When we learned she was pregnant, I was a cab driver for a company in a sleepy upstate New York community and earning less than $20,000 a year. This wasn't by design, really. As is the case with many people in the same boat, my behaviors while I was still in active addiction led to my losing every decent job I'd ever had.

The idea to drive a truck was an organic outgrowth of several different sources. I did know several guys from Narcotics Anonymous who drove trucks for a living, but I didn't think to look into it seriously until the day I was driving a medical taxi customer to an appointment and took notice of all the tractor trailers on the New York State Thruway. I knew if we were really going to start a family, I'd need to make more money, and it occurred to me that truck drivers made a lot more than I did. Let's be honest: most seventeen-year-olds working at Chick-fil-A were making more than I was at that point.

My taxi company's contract with Medicaid specified that we wait for the patient to have their doctor's appointment before driving them back home, so I spent that hour on my phone googling everything I could to find out about commercial driving schools. The information I could get was limited to basic advertising that the various schools were doing, but it was enough to get my wheels turning, so to speak. I'm not too sure I thought about anything else all day.

Later that night at the local NA meeting, I started to grill the guys who drove trucks about everything I could think of. Where did they go to school? How did they pay for the school? What were they earning? Was it hard? Did they think I could do it? My enthusiastic interviews were met with a series of grunts that — I'm not trying to be funny — reminded me a lot of how my older brother explained sex to me when I was ten years old. I got the basic, fundamental knowledge, but I was pretty much on my own when it came to filling in the details.

This is part of what makes you so fortunate for picking up this book. There is a thing in the world of self-improvement and self-help called *modeling*. Modeling is when you take information that took someone years upon years to put together, and you find a way to own this knowledge in minutes. Modeling cuts huge chunks of time off your journey to improving your life because you don't have to go through the arduous process of trial and error. Someone already did. In this case, that'd be me.

You're welcome.

Now pay close attention. The following information is going

to assist you in the process of going from $300 or $400 per week to $1,000. That's $1,000 net — you know, after the government takes their $400 cut.

Here are the very practical steps to making it happen:

1. At the end of this book, in the Appendix starting on page 177, you will find a list of state-funded programs for vocational grants set aside for people with disabilities (this means you). Find your state, and call that number to get further assistance.
2. Show up on time for all your appointments.
3. Jump through the endless array of hoops they will make you jump through — this may include interviews with your doctor, their doctor, a psychologist, and/or a certified drug counselor; a drug test; and a written test of your suitability. There is no such thing as a free lunch, but if you know what you are doing, you can get a drastically reduced lunch. Commercial driving school costs about $7,000, so think of all this crap you have to do as a temporary part-time job that pays $150 per hour.

My experience with getting the funding for commercial driving school was not unique, but it was still very interesting. The first thing I was required to do was to show up at a vocational rehabilitation "open house" at the Department of Social Services. This can be humbling, because you'll be in a room with a ton of people who have different disabilities, and if you struggle with any kind of oversize ego, which a lot of us do, your first thought will be that you don't belong. You might start to compare yourself with everyone else and come to some conclusion that you're in the wrong place. When you see the person with cerebral palsy and the other one with severe intellectual limitations, you might start to view yourself in an unfavorable light. The first thought I remember having is that I was just a guy who couldn't stop using. Maybe I should leave.

There is a spectrum when it comes to disabilities. Some people are challenged with ailments that don't improve just by the simple act of making a decision that they want them to. It is a terribly sad reality, but just because alcohol/substance abuse exists at the other end of this spectrum doesn't delegitimize how serious it is. If you consider it carefully, addiction issues are often more fatal than some of the other disabilities in the room. Don't let it psych you out. Besides, once that two-hour meeting is over, you will generally have an interview with a case worker.

My case worker was an old guy named Dave who explained that he was going to send me to speak to a credentialed alcoholism and substance abuse counselor (CASAC) at one of their affiliated outpatient rehabilitation programs. The purpose of this meeting was for the CASAC worker to determine my fitness for commercial driving school. In other words, they wanted to make sure that I did, in fact, have a substance issue and that I had been successfully abstaining for long enough to warrant their financial assistance.

I was kind of lucky. A few years earlier, I got into trouble at the car dealership where I was working, and the management sent me to this very rehab center in an attempt to comply with their Employee Assistance Program. I subsequently wound up blowing it and becoming a taxi driver, but there were records of my having attended, and it helped my case. The counselor could tell just from looking at me that I hadn't used for quite a while. He administered the obligatory saliva test and gave me the green light.

One week later, I was contacted by someone from Adult

Career and Continuing Education Services–Vocational Rehabilitation (ACCES-VR) and invited to come back for another appointment. This was the biggie. I was interviewed and asked to fill out various forms, and by the end, I was informed that my case worker would be contacting the school and setting up payment with them. I was in!

This entire process, from start to finish, took a couple of months, but it was obviously worth all the trouble. Not only did it lead to my learning the skills for a new career, but it opened up a new chapter in my life that I never saw coming. The thought that at the age of forty-two, I'd be living in the sleeper compartment of a rig and driving everywhere from Laredo to Chicago was freaky and not at all what I'd expected when I walked through those church doors two years earlier.

Now I totally get it if truck driving is not for you. As I stated in the earlier chapters, it really wasn't for me, either. In the United States, we have many federally funded job programs that will also help you get hooked up as an apprentice at over one hundred different occupations — some of them are real money earners once you're up and running. If I, personally, had had a little more than a nine-month window to drastically improve my life, I might have taken an apprenticeship in carpentry, masonry, diesel mechanics, electrical work, or plumbing — all of which pay excellent money and are open to both men and women. If you need to get the dough rolling in fast, nothing beats the ol' tractor-trailer game. If you're a single mom or there are other reasons why you can't just pack up and take to the road, keep in mind that the possibilities are virtually endless.

Side Gigs

Another consideration you'll want to keep in mind is how you will pay your bills while you are in the educational phase of your process. Originally, when I first enrolled in commercial driving school — which held classes in the daytime — I drove a cab at night. I made my rent, but I was also living on a daily ration of five hours' sleep. I would not recommend this for anyone. Don't get me wrong, though: I wouldn't discourage anyone from doing crazy things, either. Lord knows, we all did crazier shit in the name of copping and scrounging. If you have put together a little clean time and have gotten accustomed to your newfound sanity, there are other ways to creatively pay your rent while you are leveling up.

One day, I was at my friend Roxanne's apartment, and she was completely stressed-out. Not only was she moving, but the landlord had just been over there and all but promised that she would not be getting any of her $800 security deposit back. He told her the place was "trashed," and he'd need at least $800 to get it back to the condition where someone would want to rent it. In reality, it just reeked of cigarettes and had some wall damage. In a stroke of brilliance, I asked her if she'd give me some of her security deposit if I could get it back for her. She told me to take my best shot, and whatever I could get back for her, she'd split.

A little spackle and a coat of paint was all that was needed to return the place to its original…*um*…luster. The landlord had no choice but to cough up the dough. After expenses, I made $350 for half a day's work. I happen to live in a college town where people are always moving, so I was fortunate enough to turn this into a bit of a side gig, helping people prep for a move two or three times a month. I'm sure you get where I'm going with this: there is an endless fountain of little money-making opportunities that you could get involved in while you are in your transition phase, if you are resourceful enough to be open to them.

Here are some viable side hustles that you could try. Even if none of them will work for your individual situation, perhaps just reading this will kick off some ideas of your own:

1. **Drive for Uber or Lyft.** Skip to the next one if you don't have an insured vehicle or if the vehicle you do have looks like you just hit a deer and forgot to take the wreck in to the body shop. For everyone else this can be a great source of side income. I have a few friends who ran into some financial difficulties and started doing this in their free time. Near as I can tell, they averaged seventy-five to a hundred dollars per day after expenses.

2. **Sell tech services on Fiverr.** If you are in your twenties, thirties, or forties, sometimes you forget how much more you know about tech than many people in their fifties, sixties, or seventies. Can you build a website on Bandzoogle or Squarespace? How about helping someone get an e-class put together in Kajabi? If not, is it possible for you to learn fast enough to help someone out? Get creative! Spend some time brainstorming about all the tech talents you have that you might take for granted. Just because it's something everyone in your squad can do, that doesn't mean a thing. Grandpa Joe down the street is not in your crew and would probably pay you to handle something for him.

3. **Deliver food.** If you live in Ottumwa, Iowa, this isn't for you, but if you live in or around New York City, Chicago, Charlotte, Phoenix, or pretty much anywhere that can be considered even somewhat

urban, this one is great! In a nutshell, it's food delivery, and if you hustle, you can make some substantial side money with it. I'm most familiar with Postmates (postmates.com), but DoorDash, Grubhub, and Uber Eats are also options.

4. **Do odd jobs.** We all know Craigslist can be iffy at times — as a matter of fact, googling "Craigslist" ensures you will see a half dozen newspaper stories about all sorts of grimy and creative frauds born from this site. But if you look way at the bottom right-hand side of the home page for your area, there will be a box called "gigs." This, from what I gather, is the last vestige of unadulterated opportunity that Craigslist still offers. There are writing gigs, short stints at various local events, and even a few yard-work and pet-sitting positions. TaskRabbit is another site that connects freelance laborers with people who need help with household tasks — furniture delivery and assembly, laundry services, minor repairs, hauling, hanging pictures, you name it. Give it a look-see.

5. **Proofread.** If you're like me and you get a little wigged out when you see *there* being used when it should clearly be *their*, proofreading might be your calling. Go to the website freelancer.com, sign up, and start looking for work. Last I looked, there was plenty of it available, and with the convenience of the internet, obviously where you live doesn't matter at all.

6. **Walk dogs.** You can buy a fairly inexpensive advertisement on Facebook if you know what you're doing. Some helpful hints are to target just your

town and make it for one day. Doing this, I was able to get in front of five thousand sets of eyes, and it cost me about thirty dollars. I can't promise what sort of outcome you'll wind up with, but even if you can get a half of one percent of those people interested, that's twenty-five potential customers. Hook up with even half of *them*, and you'll have a nice chunk of change and a lot of new four-legged friends.

7. **Detail cars.** As a person who has been on both sides of this particular endeavor — meaning, I have made some good money doing it about ten years ago and would pay someone good money to do it for me right at this moment — I can vouch for the usefulness of this idea and the demand for this service. Word of mouth is all it takes. Almost everyone owns a car, and half of those people have children. Need I say more?

If none of these seem perfectly cut out for you, sit down and make a list of all your different skill sets. Think back to your most recent job. What things were you really great at? Once you are in possession of this list, do a little Google research and see where those talents can earn you some cash without requiring you to cough up a bunch of start-up capital. Realistically, just the act of writing out a list and spending some quality time with a search engine should kick off a stream of thoughts. It works much like the reticular activating system I explained in chapter 2. You're programmed to begin looking for opportunities, and before long they will appear.

PART

2

KICK UP YOUR FAITH
IN THE UNIVERSE

CHAPTER FIVE

Get Your Attraction On!

If you've never had children or weren't in the delivery room when the blessed event of birth has taken place, try to imagine the feeling of looking at that magical being with a face that looks just like yours. For me, that moment was overwhelming and beautiful. I was reduced to tears. All three times. After experiencing that, I found it impossible to deny the existence of *universal intelligence*. Universal intelligence is also the thing that is responsible for that first day after a long and brutal winter when you walk outside and birds are chirping, the air is bathwater warm, and the squirrels are running around manically.

I have a few friends who say they don't believe in a higher power or universal intelligence, and I don't really hold that against them. For myself, though, I just can't see this stuff as some freak cosmic accident. It's too perfect.

If you have stumbled through the doors of a 12-step program with a less-than-enthusiastic idea of whatever a higher power is, then you know the drill: you are entitled to call this thing whatever you want, as long as you are down with the fact that something bigger than you exists. Call it the universe, source energy, God, or universal intelligence — *something* out there is unexplainable.

I remember sitting in a meeting during my 90 in 90. (A *90 in 90*, for those not in the know, is the name for the very important 12-step suggestion of going to a meeting every single day for your first three months.) Everybody was taking turns talking about what God or the universe looked like or felt like to them, until some crotchety old-timer raised his hand and made the very earth-shattering point that if it's something we can understand or put our finger on, so to speak, it ceases to be Godlike. Something as powerful as this shouldn't be able to be explained by humans. His share made a huge impression on me.

I mean, think about people like Albert Einstein, John Lennon, and Marie Curie. What made them so special? They were, after all — at least neurologically — just like you and me. We are all born with the same type of brain. My gut feeling is all three had one special thing in common: they were connected very deeply to universal intelligence.

If your default settings are rooted in things like gratitude, joy, and love, you are connected deeply to source energy. Conversely, if you spend a lot of your time soaking in negative emotions, like fear, resentment, and anxiety, your connection is probably as crusty and gross as the battery terminals in a '95 Chevy Cavalier.

If this happens to be you, you have nothing to fear. It is not as difficult as you might think to join those of us on the other side.

There is an immutable law of nature referred to as the *law of attraction*. Many people who consider themselves grounded, realistic, and intelligent critical thinkers have a difficult time believing the law of attraction. I can appreciate this skepticism. I, too, roll my eyes when I overhear someone going on about mysticism and "magical thinking." I have no time for New Age woo-woo.

Allow me, however, to assist you in the separation of the *woo* from the *whoa*!

The movie *The Secret* really got to me in some ways. You could *never* convince me that anyone could possibly manifest a Maserati by staring at their hands every day and concentrating real hard, imagining them wrapped around the leather steering wheel of one. If you haven't put it together yet, I am a skeptical kid from Long Island who stumbled into middle age. But I do believe entirely in the process of being able to manifest your own reality by setting an intention for something, and I have seen material proof of this in my own life.

Let's start with the concept of gratitude. It's nearly impossible for anything positive to come into the life of a person with little or no gratitude. Gratitude, it has been proved for centuries, is the key to all things that are awesome.

When you begin your day by taking an inventory of all the things you are thankful for, you inevitably invite in more things to be thankful for. At the same time, it is practically a given that if you lie around thinking about your debts, you will perpetuate more debt. If you live in resentment about your ex-lovers, parents, stepparents, and siblings, you'll find that you will never run out of things to be resentful about. A shitty state of mind only manifests more shit.

This may sound a little tough at first. We have too many thoughts in our heads to keep an eye on every one of them.

Researchers theorize that the average human has anywhere between 50,000 and 70,000 thoughts every day. If you've ever tried to keep your eye on two coworkers — or even two cats, for that matter — you know it can be a challenge. So, how are we supposed to watch out for 50,000 *anything*?

There's a shortcut, of course: *If you can have control over your emotions, you can have control over your thoughts.* In my own life, some pretty spooky situations have convinced me of this.

A couple of years ago, things between my girlfriend and me were spinning out of control. At this point, we had two daughters, ages one and three. I was trying so hard to work on that relationship. I'd ask her continually if she'd be willing to go to a counselor, I'd talk to my sponsor, I'd share about it at meetings — but nothing was working. It was creating a lot of inner turmoil for me. As I said, my dream was to be a responsible father this time around. When we started our family, I always felt like as long as I was staying positive and sober there was nothing she and I couldn't get through.

I was starting to wonder if that were true.

Meanwhile, living with her in that situation was causing me to carry negativity around with me, against my own will. I had immersed myself in motivational books and podcasts for years, but I just could not fight the terrible feelings I had every day.

That negativity brought about more negativity. I walked into work one morning — just as I had for years — and I was called into the office. I was told that I'd backed into a loading dock of a supermarket too hard the day before and the supermarket was claiming $60,000 in building damages. My company had no other choice but to let me go.

I walked out to my car, realizing that what had just happened was truly preposterous. There wasn't any damage to the loading dock, but I was just a worker up against two large corporate entities — the trucking company and the supermarket chain — so that was that. Things, as you might imagine, really felt as though they were spiraling out of control.

The next night, I woke up at 2 AM with stabbing back pains. I wasn't sure what to do. I did not feel close enough to my girlfriend to wake her up and ask for help, so I drove myself to the emergency room. They did a CAT scan and determined that I had a kidney stone.

As I lay there in triage, I reflected back to my using days. After six years clean, there I was, alone in the hospital. I was circling the drain with my home life, but I wasn't ready to give up on it yet. The doctors gave me a prescription to help me get rid of the kidney stone, and I went home.

I learned a few days later that my health insurance had been taken away from me the very day I was terminated from my job, and the hospital visit — which cost $4,500 — was going to have to be paid out of pocket.

A week or two later, I was back at the doctor with a different set of symptoms. I was referred to the very sexy-sounding colorectal specialist. I was forty-six years old, and I felt like my body was turning against me. I couldn't understand it. For so many years, I'd lived like a total maniac and gotten away with it — sniffing, smoking, drinking, swallowing anything and everything within the vicinity of my face. Now, here I was, a clean, sober, nonsmoking vegetarian, and I felt like I was at a different doctor every other day.

I was milling around my youngest daughter's birthday party when a friend of mine came over to commiserate with me about my kidney-stone adventure. He went into unnecessary detail about how he'd also woken up in the middle of the night with stabbing pains, and he immediately woke up his wife and they packed the kids in the car and rushed to the hospital.

The story made me realize the significance of driving myself to the emergency room.

I realized my relationship with my children's mother was missing something integral. I wasn't certain it could even be addressed with counseling or therapy. There comes a time — albeit a very sad one — when a person in this kind of situation needs to come to terms with the fact that if they're pinning their happiness on the off chance that someone else might change, they are going to be unhappy for a very long time.

I wanted to be loved in the kind of way where I'd feel fine about waking up my partner and asking for help. As it was, I knew not to do that. It's one thing to *know* you would be rejected and something else to actually have to experience it.

By the time that winter was over, I'd explained to my girlfriend that I had to move out. I didn't see any other choice. It became clear to me how to work a program of recovery with regard to relationships with others. There was no arguing, no fighting, no lawyers, no court — just two adults with children coming to an agreement on how to end a relationship that was no longer functional.

So as winter gave way to springtime, I moved into a small apartment in New Paltz, a place that held profound meaning for me. This was where my parents had taken me to look at the college I eventually began attending in 1990, before any of my substance issues began to surface. Later, in 1993, this was where I started my first serious band. We played live and recorded on and off for close to twenty years. New Paltz was also where I'd met practically every woman I ever fell in love with. Some sixth sense told me that if I wanted rebirth, this was the place to be.

I was right, too. One morning a few months later, as I was walking down Main Street to get some breakfast, I felt my connection to universal intelligence reawaken. It was as if no time had elapsed since I was a hopeful kid with a bunch of wild dreams and an old guitar. I ducked into the drugstore, bought a new notebook, and headed right back to my little one-room bachelor pad.

I opened the notebook and began to plan a perfect life for myself with the premise that anything was possible — because that is exactly how I felt. My first idea was that I would take the hazmat endorsement test at the Department of Motor Vehicles, so I could be eligible for getting a higher-paying union trucking job. These jobs were the best because they paid hourly instead of by the mile. Not only that, but they offered time-and-a-half overtime pay after eight hours on any given workday.

My second plan was to start writing and publishing articles in all my favorite online magazines. I knew that if I got enough of a readership, it would be easier to get a publishing deal for the book I wanted to write. I also wanted to get myself a great life coach to help keep me on track and turn these goals into reality.

A part of me felt like I had no business making such far-reaching goals for myself. I was in my forties, unemployed, and paying child support on three kids. If I had thought about those hurdles at the time, I would never have written those things in that notebook.

This proves what I am saying. A universal intelligence helped me find a path to what I needed to focus on. This stuff really does work.

It took a month before I had my hazmat endorsement. That test was not easy. Six weeks later, I landed that union job. Again, not easy. They rejected me the first time, but I called their corporate headquarters to find out why. That was a really good idea, because they had incorrect information on me, and when I corrected this, they invited me in for an interview.

There's a really important lesson here. In the past, it would have been my style to think, *You don't want me? Yeah, well, I don't want you, either.* I believe that this is an endemic anthem for the addict. Had I taken that usual approach, nothing that is currently happening in my life would be happening. Chances are, you wouldn't even be reading this book. Looking back, I was doing so many things that I normally wouldn't be doing, and getting such incredible results. The whole thing snowballed, in a good way. One good move — the notebook — led to another, which in turn led to another.

As all of this was happening, I was playing the movie *The Secret* on my laptop every night as I went to sleep. I realize this sounds like total insanity, but to this day, I am sure the ideas in that movie became embedded in my subconscious, and allowed me to believe that anything was possible.

Within six months of getting my first article accepted by the magazine *Elephant Journal,* I was writing for them regularly. Some of my articles were even going viral — a lot of them reaching 30,000 to 40,000 views. I was so excited to be alive that after a while, I was waking up hours before work to write and exercise and meditate. My health problems disappeared as if they had never even existed in the first place.

No one could ever convince me that our minds don't control our bodies. Ironically, my union job supplies me with the greatest health insurance available, and I haven't had to use it.

Let's cut to the chase: I am sitting in my apartment — a bigger one now — writing this book because my literary agent helped me get a deal with a publisher. Every single thing I imagined for myself came true because I left that notebook open on my kitchen table and read that little essay every morning. I drank my coffee and let myself get emotionally attached to the dreams I'd planned for myself.

I managed to bounce back from getting fired and found a job that far exceeded the position I lost, and there was no reason in the world why I couldn't accomplish everything else on that page. Now I have.

All I needed to make it come true? An overwhelming sense of certainty that it would.

So, let's summarize, shall we?

1. The law of attraction is as real as life on Earth.
2. The quality of our lives is directly in line with the quality of our thoughts.
3. If we can control our emotions, we can control our thoughts — and thereby control our lives.

So, now we are left with the very real question: How do we control our emotions? If you are in recovery, or even just know you need to be, then it's clear that you already know how to control your emotions.

As a matter of fact, every single person in the back of an ambulance getting pumped full of Narcan tonight, every belligerent drunk getting beat up in a back alley, and every lonely person staring at a laptop and masturbating knows how to control their emotions.

The challenge with all these poor people is that their methods are either fatal or just plain awful.

Hopefully, this all changes after we get into recovery and begin to live differently. Instead of using substances, alcohol, or porn, we learn to call our sponsor or a friend or read recovery literature.

Usually, any of these methods will work for us. However, it is also important that we learn how to change our state when none of these options are available. Personally speaking, there have been times when I've been faced with uncomfortable feelings and I couldn't get to a meeting, no one was picking up the phone, and reading was out of the question. In these moments, we cannot afford to allow ourselves to be swallowed up by negativity.

Here's a four-step technique that will work:

1. **Figure out exactly what you are feeling.** If the first thing that pops into your mind is "pissed," stop for a second. "Pissed" is an umbrella term for a lot of different feelings. You'll want to isolate the exact feeling as best as you can. Did your boyfriend say something to you that made you feel inferior or less than? Did your boss insult you and cause you to fear the loss of your job and your income? Get quiet for a second and figure out exactly how you feel.

2. **Honor the emotion.** Fear is not a useless emotion. It is a signal from our brain that informs us we need to be prepared for an upcoming challenge. Guilt isn't useless, either. It is a message that we have violated something important inside ourselves. If you take a second and think about why you are feeling what you are feeling, it will give you a great opportunity to get to the root cause. That will, in turn, make it that much easier to get past it.

3. **Decide what you'd like to feel instead.** You might be thinking, *Happy, stupid!* Expand on that a little. Do you want to go from anxiety to a state

of calm? Do you want to stop feeling sad and feel joyous instead? It's a good idea to focus on what it is you are trying to accomplish. It's obvious we'd all like to feel better. The real question is: Better how?

4. **Take action.** The final step is action. What the action should be depends on what the negative emotion is. If you felt rejected by your girlfriend, let her know how you feel. If you don't have your rent and you are stuck in anxiety, go talk to your landlord and get it handled. *These suggestions sound so obvious, but just because a thing seems obvious doesn't mean we always pay attention to it.* I know even *I* get overwhelmed sometimes and feel so paralyzed, I forget to do anything about the problem. That makes the issue fester and get worse.

Using this technique regularly will help you stay in a place of love, gratitude, and joy — and as I said, these emotions will keep your thoughts where they need to be in order to attract all the good things into your life. This is the reason I felt compelled to share the story of my recent breakup. That situation was an honest look at how differently the same life can be experienced, based solely on the thoughts a person has from day to day. In this case, the person happened to be me.

I want you to do a great exercise, usually called the BPS exercise. BPS stands for "Best Possible Self." What you will do is exactly what I did when I ducked into that drugstore and bought that notebook on my fateful jobless morning.

Imagine your best possible self.

Pick up your pen and at the top of the page write *Best Possible Self*, so you'll have no problem finding this page later, as it works best if you look at it every single day. This is similar to the exercise on page 14 of chapter 1, which you did on the second page of your notebook, except now we are really going for it. In present tense, as if it is already happening, write a story of how you see yourself. Where are you living? Who are you living with? Do you have a beautiful dog? A yard?

If I had to boil down the essence of this chapter, it would be to convince you that if I can be here writing this book — something that was only the spark of a dream not too long ago — then you could be doing anything, too.

Don't get caught up in inhibitions, and don't filter your thoughts through any screen of realism.

If your dream is to learn to play the piano and sing, write it down. Or maybe you want to start working as an extra on movie sets. Or open a construction business. It's all possible.

Also, don't forget to leave the notebook in a conspicuous spot every day. The most important part of this exercise is to keep these visions up front. With life as it usually is, it can be very easy to get caught up in basic minutiae and forget about your lofty goals. You cannot allow that to happen. Nothing kills human potential faster than getting caught up in the minor inconveniences of survival.

Like I've said all along, keep reading through these exercises every day. If you're stumped or having a difficult time with this exercise, read chapter 6 and then try it again. If you can get some clarity about your calling, it might make your BPS exercise more attainable.

CHAPTER SIX

Find Your Calling

The process of creating a compelling life has many moving parts, for anyone — and even more so for someone in recovery. Attracting positive people and situations, as we discussed in the last chapter, is a crucial part of it, but it usually doesn't work all by itself. We need to create a viable plan and set real goals for our lives in order to gain enough force to get the wheels turning. However, before we go about the business of putting together that particular cart, we need to have a horse to put in front of it. In other words, we can't just pick random goals for ourselves. To be honest, we can't pick goals based on anything other than what we feel we've been put on this planet to do.

And, yes, I realize I have spent quite a bit of time extolling the virtues of raising yourself up to earning $1,000 per week, but make sure you understand the entire purpose behind *Kick-ass Recovery*. You are going to get sick of driving a truck. Or hammering nails. Or turning a wrench. Once you have observed yourself conquering the impossible dream — once you have raised yourself up to a point where you are making three times what you are used to earning — you're not going to want to stop there.

As someone who has been driving a truck for over six years now, I cannot stress enough the *importance of expansion*. For human beings, the novelty of earning any amount of money has an expiration date. Our tastes and our spending habits naturally change after a while, and we may find ourselves right back in the same rut we were in years earlier — just with a different-looking W2 come tax season. So, it's best not to allow yourself to get too comfortable in one spot for too long. It's totally natural for you to find yourself daydreaming on your way to work: *If I was able to accomplish that, who's to say that I couldn't do* _____ [fill in the blank]?

That very real desire and longing inside you can lead to some wonderful things happening in your life. That very thing is likely what led to you read this book. That is why it's so important that you find your calling.

Transforming your life — from something that feels *meh* into something that excites the hell out of you — takes that special something. That intangible thing inside us that makes us do the seemingly impossible. Like when we got into recovery and began this incredible and scary sober life in the first place — but that's my point. That very thing that you need in order to make this happen *already lives inside you*. You've tapped into it a few times already, and now you need to access it again to find your calling.

Merriam-Webster's Dictionary defines the word *calling* as "a strong inner impulse toward a particular course of action especially when accompanied by conviction of divine influence."

When you break down that definition, you realize that we are, once again, in the realm of the big stuff. Divine influence, universal intelligence, higher power, God, the universe — call it whatever you want, but it is crucial that we all understand that when we have the privilege to connect to that very thing we feel we've been put on this planet to do, we become unstoppable. This is a universal truth. At least on a subconscious level, we all know what our calling is, but sometimes it takes a little digging — or a clearing away of the mounds of unhelpful garbage that we've collected over the years — to discover it.

The problem we face is that we are subjected to outside influences from the time we are first conscious of our surroundings — and as you can perhaps attest, these are often not the most ideal surroundings.

When I was twenty-three years old, I was the leader of one of the coolest bands in my college town. This was before the internet, so the social scene was quite different at the time. Guys and girls hung out at the corner deli, and when they got bored of that, they'd move in little packs from one person's apartment to the next to smoke cigarettes and make out with whomever they were dating that week. Regular kid stuff.

My apartment always had a healthy draw because our friends knew there would be live music, cute girls hanging around, and all the drama that goes along with that. There was also that searing energy in the air that usually comes as a result of four guys who are in it to win it. In addition to all this, we were always writing new music and recording it on our multi-track recorder, and we were always quite liberal about sharing our new material with our friends. These cassettes would get copied dozens of times, and the songs were usually known all over town. We were also booked at the various college bars and clubs every weekend.

One particular weekend stands out in my memory more than any other. My mother and father were planning to make the three-hour drive to come visit me and see our band play, and I was buzzing with excitement. Not so much to see my parents, but for my parents to see how adored I was by the townspeople, the college girls, the street kids, and my bandmates.

My entire childhood, as you may recall, was a study in alienation. The thought that my mother and father were going to see me in this new environment — which in the past had been the stuff of only my most secret desires and daydreams — had me just bursting at the seams.

Finally, I kept thinking. *They are going to understand what I have believed all along — that there is something great about me. Something special they've never paid attention to.*

For everyone else in my band, the week leading up to that gig was like any other. It was a lot of hanging around and navel-gazing in the band room. (I use the term *band room*, but what it was, in reality, was my bass player Chris's bedroom. Where most people prefer to have a bed, a nightstand, and a bookshelf, he was quite content to have all our equipment set up to play at a moment's notice and a sleeping bag in the corner on the off chance he might want to crash once in a while.) These band activities also included intermittent fits and starts of running through our set and experimenting with different combinations of songs to keep the pace of our show running smoothly. To me, though, this week was very different. I was holding back on my singing so I could have every ounce of my voice available to me for the night my parents were going to be there. I even changed my guitar strings — which in those days usually only happened one string at a time as they broke. So, I was really pulling out all the stops.

The big night arrived, and things could not have gone

better. My band was the headliner, and the people in the club were going nuts — clapping, screaming my name. I couldn't possibly have asked for my friends to be more supportive. My band was tight and we sounded great, and I could not wait to get off the stage and soak in all the acclaim I was going to receive from my parents, who had been so stingy with it all my life.

I sat down at their table, ostensibly to greet them but in reality to enjoy this incredible moment. My dad looked at me and smiled. My mother giggled and looked back at my father.

"What did you say, hun...?" She laughed. "There's an ass —"

"There's a seat for every ass," he corrected her, looking at my mother and then at me, preparing to revel in all the laughter he was expecting to get.

I am sharing this tale of flawless parenting with you for the express purpose of helping you understand that this was the way a lot of us were "encouraged" by our loved ones. And we need to do the work required to shake off all that negativity, especially those of us who left our childhood homes and set out to spend the rest of our lives proving everyone wrong, the way I did.

Here are some great exercises for helping you zero in on what your calling might be if you are having trouble figuring it out. But even if you feel like you are completely in touch with your innermost longings, read on anyway. Some of these exercises might help even *you*, my levelheaded reader, to create better distinctions.

Step #1: Think Like an Alien

If an alien beamed down to Earth and saw you, you can probably imagine that they would be viewing you without any preconceived notions. Think about it: if that alien walked into the club over twenty years ago, on that night I just described, and needed to make some kind of report about it, the words *ass* and *seat* would not make it into the report. Those observations are completely irrelevant and are only the kind of thing a human with all the biases that come with having known you since you were an infant — and who cannot see your full potential — would consider. So, this is how you must try to see yourself: the same way an alien without preconceived notions would see you.

Let me show you how it's done by using the analogy of my personal story: The alien would notice that I love to perform. The alien would observe that other people love watching me perform. Given that information, the Great Gazoo would write a glowing report of my entertainment value back to his contingent on the planet Zorch.

So, what would Gazoo say if he spent the week observing *you* without having been exposed to the opinions of your parents, siblings, or your own toxic self-talk? Are you great at building stuff? Listening and giving helpful advice to others? Nurturing children? Any of those talents could be cultivated into an exciting future. Whether you decide to go on and open your own daycare facility or a coaching service, just remember — the sky is the limit! You may not feel that way initially, and the people around you may have their doubts, but if Gazoo sees it, it is true.

Step #2: Remember What You Loved to Do as a Kid

Think about all the fantasies you've had since forever but have always been too scared to take seriously. There's gold in there if you tell yourself it's okay to entertain those fantasies. Take out your notebook and write down a list of everything that used to get you jazzed as a kid. Don't leave anything out, either. It will all help you to get to that pot of gold known as "your calling."

When I was a kid, there was a television show called *Lou Grant*. It was a spin-off of the ancient sitcom *The Mary Tyler Moore Show*. There must have been geniuses involved in the show's creation because, somehow, they managed to make working on a newspaper seem cool and edgy. Its magic must have relied heavily on the times, because now it all kind of seems ridiculous. I tried to watch a few episodes recently on YouTube, and honestly, it is as seventies as bell bottoms and the Bee Gees — but what can I say? I'm middle-aged.

Still, when I was a kid and that show was current, it would cause me to daydream about what it might be like to some-day be an investigative reporter for a newspaper. The idea of going into work with my cup of coffee and tap-tap-tapping away on a typewriter made my heart race a little. And that, as you can see, just happens to be exactly what I am doing right now: sipping a cup o' joe and tap-tap-tapping away on my key-board! Writing is what gets me out of bed and running toward the coffeemaker every morning. It's what keeps me up late at night.

So, what used to get you excited? Did you love to watch Olympic gymnasts? Hockey games? MMA guys beating the crap out of each other? As seemingly unimportant as these answers appear, you must spend some time writing them all down. If you really put some thought into it, any of these examples might start pointing you in the direction of becoming a personal trainer or opening your own toddler gym or a hockey rink for teenagers. It's all possible. Once you decide that there are no limits to what you can do, *there really are no limits*. It's that simple.

Step #3: Use Your Envy

What have you seen other people doing that just makes you writhe with jealousy? Do you see guys playing guitar solos on-stage and wish that could be you? Do you see other women shining on the catwalk, or getting thousands of likes as a result of the awesome podcast they recently launched? Do you want to be an influencer or start one of those homespun do-it-your-self YouTube reality shows? Really break down what it is about the things you see on social media that gives you a visceral feeling of envy. It may not necessarily be the actual thing the people are doing but rather the rewards they are getting from what they are doing.

From there, you can go on to design and create your own world — a world that will inevitably make someone else envy *you* someday. Envy, like most emotions, has its place. Anything you can use as fuel to create something positive is useful. It's only when emotions become unhelpful or destructive that we need to be wary of them.

Step #4: Allow Yourself to Be Bored

One of the most tragic consequences of the smartphone is the fact that people have developed marked aversions to spending any more than four seconds not swiping, watching, scrolling, texting, sexting, or reading something. The problem with this is that it used to be in those uncomfortable periods of bore-dom when the most fertile creativity could be found. I would never ask you to alter your habits indefinitely, but just as an ex-periment, shut off your phone and allow yourself to be bored for a few minutes every day — like, say, while you eat lunch. It's entirely possible it may be the greatest gift you've ever given yourself.

Step #5: Don't Just Stand There — Do Something

Sometimes, your best bet is just to start *doing something* — anything, actually. I cannot tell you how many times I sat down at my computer completely out of ideas when I needed to come up with an article to write — and I just started typing whatever came into my mind. Granted, I'd generally go back and manicure the first few paragraphs once I understood the direction I was heading in, but the point is, it got me *heading in a direction.*

We, as creatures who are charged with self-preservation, cannot always be consciously plugged into our most creative thoughts. It would be difficult to eat or to avoid car accidents if we were. Sometimes, we just need to get active in order for that part of us to bubble up to the surface. If you are not consciously aware of your calling at this very second, start doing this thing and that thing — whatever comes to mind — and inevitably, it will come to you. At the very least, it will come to you a lot faster than if you sat there watching *Gilligan's Island* all day. (That is, unless your calling is to give three-hour tours from the outer banks of Honolulu.)

I knew a young woman once who was working a minimum-wage job as a home health aide but was passionate about animals. She began to do a little pet-sitting here and there for extra money. Every so often, she would get some word-of-mouth referrals but never really enough to make it a full-time occupation. What she realized, though, was that the $200 or $300 a month she was making bought her a substantial amount of Facebook advertising when she limited the demographic she targeted to only her town. This turned out to be an extremely successful venture, and at one point, she had too many requests to handle all by herself. It didn't take too long for her to go from hearing crickets to needing to find an assistant to take some of the workload from her. Talk about luxury problems, right?

The point is that she didn't spend a lot of time sitting around trying to map out the perfect game plan. She just started doing something. Taking any action at all will nearly always lead to a certain momentum that in turn will drive you toward the end zone. Sitting around and mulling things over and over again will usually lead to watching blooper reels from the second season of *The Office*. (Don't get me wrong — I love those blooper reels. But, you know. Everything has a time and a place, and all that.)

Last but Not Least: Set Goals

What if you are already painfully aware of your calling and you do not need to think like an alien? What if you remember exactly what got you juiced up as a kid, because it still gets you going today? What if you don't need to plug into your envy or start moving your body? What then?

I'm glad you asked. The good news is that setting a couple of goals will help you get *and stay* in motion. Even by just naming your goal and working out a few steps you can take now to start to achieve it, you'll already be ahead of 90 percent of the population who never even start.

When I published my first article on a popular blog site, I was flying high from the unexpected positive response the article received. I was receiving personal emails, Facebook friend requests, and Instagram followers. It pumped me so full of a new sense of purpose that the first thing I wanted to do was publish another article. This all took off so quickly that within a few months, I was asked by the editors if I'd like to consider becoming a regular contributor.

Months after that happened, I was then asked if I wanted

to be one of their featured writers. This inspired me to start making some real moves toward the planning and execution of this book. And if you really consider the actual course of events, my life began to change significantly in no time at all! This is a common occurrence when anyone starts to build a little momentum toward achieving their destiny. The trick is really to follow the thread. Allow one joyful moment to build to the next one.

We spend so much of our lives trying to desperately fit into what is happening externally, when we should be doing the exact opposite. Our greatness flourishes when we learn to take the gifts inside us and bring them to the surface. It is what author and speaker Kyle Cease referred to as "living from the inside out." This is what children do when they play. This is the thing that happens to us when we get so immersed in something that we lose track of time.

You may have noticed that when I brought up examples of talents or interests you might have, my ideas for how to use those interests were big and bad. For example, if you love gymnastics, my suggestion was to figure out a way to open your own toddler gym. Many people would probably advise you to play it safe and shoot lower. In other words, they might say that perhaps you should try to get a twelve-dollar-an-hour job as an assistant over at Ms. Gotchtalk's gymnasium, not figure out a way to open your own gym.

You are hereby *not authorized* to accept anything less than whatever gets you jumping out of bed in the morning and thanking the universe for another day. Now, don't get me wrong. If you can truly be happy, through and through, with a twelve-dollar-an-hour job at someone else's gym, then by all means, go for it! However, if you get quiet and be honest with yourself and realize that you will not be satisfied unless it's you who's running shit, then you *must* set the wheels in motion to make that happen.

Realistically speaking, there is not much more effort required in doing the big things than in doing the smaller things. If you break down everything that is required throughout the process of finding yourself a minimum-wage job — all the hoops you have to jump through to get situated in that job, plus all the stress of being a low-level employee — it is not really such a breeze. So, if you're going to be expending all kinds of energy anyway, why not focus on doing it for a greater return on your investment? For example, the return of being *completely, wildly in love with your life!*

We live in a world where resources are not always available to everyone — but *resourcefulness* is up for grabs. I am not sitting at a big oak desk in a split-level ranch in Malibu. I am sitting at a desk that I bought through Craigslist. The desk is in my one-bedroom apartment. The apartment is in a small college town in upstate New York. There is no limit to the number of people on this planet who are in possession of way more resources than I have, yet their voices will never be heard by as many people as this book will reach.

Resources without resourcefulness are, for the most part, useless. Resourcefulness, even if you have no resources at your disposal, can still open the door to all your wildest dreams. If I had to isolate the most important point of this whole chapter, this would be it. There will always be people around you who will be terribly invested in trying to convince you that you do not have what you need in order to do the "big things." I am not necessarily busting on these people. This is also what *they* have been told from the moment they came screaming into the world. It is the great lie that has been passed down from generation to generation — and quite frankly, I've always believed it to be the narrative a person uses to get free of all this "trying" stuff and get back to the important business of catching up on reality shows and sitcoms. I'm here to not only tell you but *prove to you*, through my own story, that this mindset is not just incorrect but poisonous.

The truth of the matter is that if you can rent an apartment, you can rent a storefront. If you can rent a storefront, you can sell people the things they want. I mean, somebody's doing it. There is no reason in heaven or on Earth why that person cannot be you. You, my friend, are a rockstar!

Extra Credit

If you feel like you might want to take this "finding your calling" thing to the next level, check out Julia Cameron's *The Artist's Way*. It is a twelve-week course of exercises you can use to tap into your repressed creative side. The "Morning Pages," an exercise in which you write stream-of-consciousness style at the beginning of your day, has helped millions of people uncover things about themselves that they might have never realized otherwise.

CHAPTER SEVEN

Rehearse Happiness

W alk down any city block, meandering like a tourist, and
the locals will — in silent and subtle fashion — push
you out of their way. You'll find yourself on the outskirts of
their sidewalk territory. Move through that same city block
knowing exactly where you're headed, and people will subconsciously move right out of *your* way.

It is the way of the world. You have to do the same thing
with your life.

Once you have made a decision to do something — *anything* — the world begins to look different. This only works,
though, if you truly understand the meaning of the word *decision*. Don't roll your eyes. Of course it's an easy word, but stop
being a know-it-all for a second and listen up!

Check this out. The word *decision* is a lot like the word
incision, as I pointed out in chapter 2. *Incision* usually refers
to a surgeon cutting into you; *decision* means you cut away all

other options except the one you have chosen. For example, deciding to get sober means you do not spend any time day-dreaming about how nice a glass of Prosecco might taste. That doesn't even come on your radar as an option. You cut away that idea. Keep cutting away anything that detracts from the decision you've made.

Another side effect of a true decision: action usually follows immediately. When my girlfriend and I decided we were going to start a family, I got right on the phone with the commercial driving school and asked them to send me a brochure. I wasn't entirely certain at first how I was going to pay for the school or how I'd manage to attend and work enough to pay my rent and bills, but I did not let that get in my way. I moved like a dude stepping off the train to head right for the 2nd Avenue Deli for a pastrami sandwich. Everything, I can assure you, got out of my way.

Later on, I worked out the obstacles of driving a cab at night, going to school during the day, getting the tuition from ACCES-VR, actually getting my girlfriend pregnant — there were many steps to the process. But as I have brought up a few times so far, I have the truck-driving job, and there are two little girls fighting over one desk chair in the next room — so the plan came together pretty well, if I do say so myself.

The trick to all this comes down to what you decide to focus on.

I could have easily focused on the difficulties of being a completely broke person trying to go to a full-time school while still paying rent, since that was my reality. I might still be sitting at the taxi stand explaining to anyone who would listen that I could have had a really cool life, if only someone would have let me crash on their couch for a couple of months while I learned how to drive a truck. I didn't focus on that, though.

Obviously, I focused on what I needed to do to make it happen. And it happened.

The management at the taxi company where I worked weren't delusional. They knew that driving a cab in the Hudson Valley region of New York was a straight dead-end proposition. When they noticed how determined I was to change my life, they changed a few things around, gave me a work shift that accommodated my inconvenient schedule, and allowed me to earn a little while I learned a lot. Granted, I only slept from 2 to 7 AM six days a week, but I managed somehow.

The Precedent Effect

Now we come to a point I don't want you to forget: Once you begin to tackle the impossible, or what seemed impossible at one time, a magic thing happens inside you and you will not just stop at truck driving or plumbing or construction.

I call this the *precedent effect.*

I experienced this a lot in early recovery. Right around the time I got my six-month key tag from NA, I sat at a meeting and ran through my own personal movie in my mind, from that night when I hit the lowest bottom of my life to the present. I was filled with such incredible gratitude and pride in myself. I wanted to experience that feeling again. I wanted to stretch even more.

And so I did. A few months after I had my one-year celebration — which in and of itself was a beautiful, life-changing event — I got the equivalent of almost two months' salary together and rented my own apartment.

Amid the overflowing boxes and displaced furniture, I soaked in the joys of having my own domicile, complete with a fireplace. A year earlier, I was renting a room in a boarding-house and sometimes even had trouble coming up with the

$175 per week to do that. At one point, I asked one of my new friends from a meeting for a ride to the drugstore, and then for two dollars to buy toothpaste once we got there.

This progression was kind of earth-shattering, and I was pretty impressed. It emboldened me to try to do other things that, at first, seemed impossible up to that point. I mean, think about it: I was not using substances at all after nearly twenty years. Then I was no longer smoking cigarettes after nearly thirty years. From there on it went: girlfriend, truck-driving school, truck-driving job, daughters, publishing online, getting a book deal. Each time, I took a moment to steep in the joy of my progression.

There were even more accomplishments than that along the way, but you get the idea.

Rehearsing happiness is an essential part of the magic. You must go beyond wishing and beyond desiring. You need to put your plan into action and truly visualize the outcome. As I said in the earlier chapters, this cannot be halfhearted. You need to get emotionally attached to what you are going to create for yourself.

I started doing this early on, without even realizing the importance of what I was doing. It began when I used to sit in the NA meetings as a newcomer listening to people share their stories. I would observe the ones with substantial time in the program — their stories of the families they started, jobs they got, lives they were living — and I would imagine myself up there someday telling a story just like that.

Then when I fell in love a short time later, I imagined the two of us together. I imagined the family we would start and the things we would all do together in such vivid detail that they would appear in my dreams sometimes.

I did it, once again, when it came to this book. In the

process of trying to get this book into your hands, there were plenty of stumbling blocks and walls put up in front of me, but I kept pushing and visualizing this book on the shelf in the bookstore. I saw the cover, and I could see people buying it and reading it. I did this every day until I finally received the green light I was focused on getting.

Even after I signed the contract, obstacles kept appearing around every corner. My boss needed me to stay at work thirteen hours a day, the kids needed me to take them to Chuck E. Cheese on the weekends, plus I needed at least six hours of sleep every night, and somewhere amidst all this I had to figure out how to write this thing.

It was reminiscent of my days working my way through commercial driving school. The only difference was what I was doing. Instead of driving a cab at night and going to school during the day, I was waking up at dawn to write and driving the 12-to-12 shift.

I imagine your experience will be similar. There will be no shortage of roadblocks along the way. There will absolutely be times — maybe even once or twice a day — when you will feel tempted to throw this book in the trash and go back to whatever you are doing just to get by.

This is normal. It is also why it is so important to see the outcome clearly in your mind every day. It is going to be your only defense against the temptation of giving up when things start to look impossible.

The Science of Imagination

If I told you details about a steakhouse I used to go to in midtown Manhattan — like how upon walking through the door, you're met with sounds of clanging silverware and dishes, and the smells of sautéed onions and sizzling steak and grilled swordfish, and the sights of crispy fresh salads flying by on waiters' trays — you might start to actually salivate.

Why? Because human beings are very sensual creatures. This is why it is so important to *use all your senses in imagining yourself already having achieved your goals long before they come to fruition.* Breathe like you're already making the money that you are poised to make. Walk down the street like someone who doesn't owe anyone a dime. Head held high. Chest out. Shoulders back. Confident grin on your face.

Some quick scientific facts to explain why this is so important: Sports psychologist and Olympic coach Dr. Richard Suinn discovered that when he asked downhill skiers to visualize their competitions, their brain waves and even their muscles responded in exactly the same way as if these athletes were actually competing. Their autonomic nervous systems triggered the same responses, also. In another French Olympic study, it was proved that long-jumpers who visualized their events improved their jumping distances 45 percent of the time.

You can use goal setting the same way. Break down your plan into what you'll have to do the first week, the second week, next month. Keep track of your progress. Be visual; always picture where you want to end up. This allows you to keep on your path even when you feel like giving up.

I can't overstate the importance of going through your typical day as though you have already accomplished the goal you have set for yourself. Just as the famous Olympic trainer proved, our brains do not know the difference between something we experience in reality and something we vividly imagine, and the most effective way to convince your brain of anything is through your physiology. In other words, the way you carry your body.

A genius named Dr. Joe Dispenza made a lifelong study of

this and wrote about it extensively in a book called *Breaking the Habit of Being Yourself*. In a nutshell, he explains that just *trying* to think positively isn't enough because we have habitual patterns in our bodies that cause us to constantly have the same thoughts. The only way to truly change the way we perceive the world around us or what we choose to focus on is by changing how we use our bodies. Interesting stuff.

The Crab Mentality

I will warn you in advance, though. When you have adopted this new way of walking in the world, the people around you who are not taking this "changing your entire reality" thing seriously will start to give you a hard time. Most especially your close friends. In their confusion, they will probably try to come at you with the "Who do you think you are?" or "What, you're too good for us now?" narrative.

Do not — I repeat, *do not* — let this knock you off your game. It just means your plan is working. The longer you are on your path, and the more your life begins to improve, the more you are going to deal with this nay-saying.

As a matter of fact, you might begin to notice that the need for making different friends will arise.

As you probably remember, you had to do this when you got into recovery, too. Now, of course, it doesn't have to be nearly as drastic as it was when you had to change all your people, places, and things in your new life of sobriety. You are, however, going to have to at least limit your exposure to the crybabies, sad sacks, passive-aggressive Negative Nellies and Toxic Tommys who try to convince you to settle for a life of McDonald's and mediocrity.

You may have heard of the phenomenon known as the "crab mentality," but even if you haven't, you'll recognize it immediately. If you've ever gone crabbing or seen crabs in a bucket, you may have noticed how when one tries to climb out of the bucket, all the others grab at the escape artist and pull it back in, as if to say, "If I have to finish the night on someone's dinner plate, then so do you!" People are like crabs in this way. So, don't be baffled when you are subjected to it.

You are also completely not authorized to spend any of your precious time trying to proselytize to the "poor me" crowd. If a crab ever defied all odds and did manage to get over the rim of the bucket, how much time do you think it would spend talking to the other crabs still inside about how great it felt to be free? I imagine that crab would hide somewhere in the galley before the others realized it was gone.

You can send a good thought out into the universe, you can say a silent prayer, but in your period of transition, you cannot risk the possibility of any of these negative forces getting any stage time. They will plant the awful-smelling seeds of doubt in your brain, and all of a sudden, without even realizing it, you'll be back to walking around like someone who's broke, owes everyone money, and shouldn't even waste their time trying. Stay out of that bucket once you've gotten over the top.

I shouldn't even have to mention that the visualization trick works in both directions. That is why it is crucial to steer clear of these people as much as possible. Let us be realistic, though. You will not always be successful at this. Some of them might be family or coworkers. You're still going to have to go to work wherever you're currently employed; you're still going to have to go home every night — there's still going to be Thanksgiving dinner at your uncle Harry's. It's not a perfect world.

In these extreme cases where you cannot escape or avoid the naysayers, you will have to stand strong. A great quote attributed to Henry Ford summarizes this perfectly: "Whether you think you can or whether you think you can't — you're right."

Henry Ford would know, too. In 1928, he assembled an entire team of the most advanced engineers of his time in a room and told them he had a vision for the first workable V-8 engine. At that time, no one had managed to figure out a practical way to build a motor with eight cylinders in a single engine block. The engineers patiently listened to him for a while and then turned to each other to make sure they were all in agreement before they broke the sad news to Ford.

They declared with certainty that it could not be produced.

"Produce it anyway," Ford said.

Why am I telling you this story? For the simple reason that there will never be any shortage of people in the world who will tell you all the reasons what you are trying to do won't work. The Ford V-8 became one of the best motors of all time, once the engineers got out of their own way. That's quite a distinction for something that couldn't be produced.

I was told on countless occasions that my ideas were ridiculous. I have a vivid memory of driving to work, talking to a friend on the phone about my idea for this book. He agreed halfheartedly that it might be an okay idea, but he just couldn't see where I'd get a whole book out of it. That phone call really brought me down, because he was someone I'd looked up to since I first got into recovery. He's in the music business, and I often turned to him for advice.

Later that day, however, I realized that he was just a human being, and he didn't have to share my vision. Only *I* had to believe in me for the moment.

I've revisited this revelation many times since then when needed.

What you will find, over time, is that many people won't

start to believe in you until you've made some visible head-way. And there's nothing wrong with our friends adopting the "I'll believe it when I see it" mentality. It's a little disheartening, but it is reality sometimes. The real problem is if *we* begin to get that attitude. That's the kiss of death. We, as our own one-person fan club, need to *believe* our dreams way before we *see* any "hard proof" — or it is likely we will never see those dreams come true.

What Else Do We Need?

Okay, so a definite purpose, the strength to make a hard deci-sion, and determination are three key elements in our climb to the life we have always imagined for ourselves.

Once we have those in place, we can then add two more el-ements that will make us practically unstoppable — *persistence* and *faith*.

Persistence

We need persistence because, obviously, we need to keep trying no matter how many times we don't get it right.

It's crucial that we keep this mindset: *If I try something and it doesn't work out the way I had hoped, I did not fail — I gained a result that was different than I wanted.*

That's it. When Edison struggled to invent the lightbulb, it took him countless attempts before he figured it out. And in his later work to develop his alkaline storage battery, he con-ducted more than 10,000 experiments with different chemi-cals. Before ultimately succeeding, he told a friend, "Why, man, I have gotten lots of results! I know several thousand things that won't work!" You can use that. Edison was employing a method known as *reframing*. He decided it would be a lot more valuable to look at his experiences in an empowering way instead of a defeatist way. It most likely led to his eventual success.

Another great example of persistence can be found in the story of Colonel Harlan Sanders. If you've ever eaten at KFC, you might be interested to know that when Colonel Sanders received his first Social Security check for $105, he said, "Uh-uh. This is not how I'm riding off into the sunset."

Actually, no one really knows what he said, but the point is that he wasn't going to accept that as a retirement package. At 66 years old, he got in his car and drove around the country selling chicken franchises with nothing more than some chickens, a pressure cooker, and his old southern gift of gab.

Are you seeing a pattern?

The moral of the story is always the same: You will never fail if you never stop trying. Truthfully, most people give something a shot once or twice and then quietly go back home and grab the remote with the hope that no one even noticed. If you have the opportunity to talk to anyone who has ever accomplished something extraordinary — something beyond what most people have been able to — you will find that in more than 99 percent of these cases the person just *never gave up* until they got what they wanted.

Faith

Persistence would be close to impossible without faith. We need faith because there will be times when all the worldly evidence points to the possibility that we may be wasting our time. We are faced with one brick wall after another, and as someone who has absolutely been there, I can assure you that without faith, you very well might give up on your vision.

You simply must know in your heart that what you are

trying to do is possible, people have done it before, and it is there for you if you *just don't give up*. If you possess a burning desire for just about anything, you are already halfway to making it happen. Just look at the literal definition of the word *desire: De sire*, "Of the father." You would not have the ability to desire a thing if God did not equip you with everything you need to make it come true.

Want to really drive this point home? Get out your notebook and try these exercises:

1. Write a paragraph about what it will feel like when you are waking up every morning knowing that you have a few thousand dollars in your checking account, and a few hundred dollars in your pocket. Really close your eyes and feel it in your body. The more descriptive you can be in this paragraph, the better the chances that you will be able to make this happen. As I mentioned earlier when I explained the reticular activating system in your brain, when we commit things to paper and regularly look at what we wrote, we put our brains on the subconscious "lookout" for any and all opportunities that come near us.

2. Write a paragraph about a time in your life when you experienced the "crab mentality" firsthand. How long ago was it? How did it make you feel? How do you plan to deal with it when it happens next time?

3. Earlier in this chapter, I discussed the *precedent effect*, that awesome thing that happens when you take a moment to let it sink in just how far you have come. Can you describe a time when you experienced this?

How did it make you feel? Does it inspire you to try for even greater accomplishments?

4. What are some ways you can rehearse happiness today? How can you start to carry your body as if you already have the things you desire?

Once you have all this stuff written down, you will be in a different place emotionally and mentally.

It makes a big difference in your whole outlook when you really begin to embody the person you see yourself becoming.

CHAPTER EIGHT

Give It Up for Gratitude

You're doing your last-minute Christmas shopping, lost in deep contemplation of whom you've bought for, whom you still need to buy for, and if your aunt Theresa will think you're cheap for giving her a glazed doughnut–scented candle, and you notice someone rushing toward the door in your peripheral vision. You know that feeling you get, when you hesitate and hold the door open, not only because it's the holiday season but also because it's the right thing to do, and lo and behold, the brunette with the mink coat blasts right past you without saying thank you or making eye contact?

It really rankles your crank, doesn't it? This should give you some indication of how the universe feels when it goes through all the trouble of providing you with clean water, shelter, food, people who love you, and the ability to make coffee, and you never once utter or even allow yourself to feel the slightest bit of thankfulness.

On the other side of this coin, it has been proved time and time again that when a person lives in a state of unceasing gratitude, they never run out of things to be grateful for. Do you know any of these mysterious people who seem to have one cool thing after another happen to them? They know this secret. You, on the other hand, can start to feel grateful right now, because after you read this chapter, you will know the same secret.

I'm not sure how much you know about physics, but I'm certain at some time you've heard that everything — including you — is made up entirely of molecules. And you might have also heard that molecules are made up of atoms, unless you happened to be absent that day. What you might not know, however, is that atoms are more than 99 percent energy. Most people just assume that our bodies and everything around us are mostly matter, but this is not true. They're mostly energy.

This is why when we are engaging in high-frequency thoughts and emotions, we tend to attract more high-frequency situations into our lives, and vice versa. Don't we all know that person with the terrible attitude who never ceases to find things to complain about?

"Every day it's the same thing," he begins. "I go in to work, I get harassed by the customers — who, by the way, are coming in nonstop — and I'm stuck in that hell until six o'clock. Then I walk through the door to my house, and Jessica hands off the baby to me like she's Tom Brady, and now I've gone from Retail Ricky to Mary Poppins. The shit never ends. When do I get the time to just do me? I'm seriously just gonna bail if something doesn't change soon. Besides that...*blah*...*blah*...*blah*..."

There are so many things this person fails to realize. Yes, eight hours a day in retail can suck, but he's not working in a sweatshop in Bangladesh for *sixteen* hours a day or staving off severe malnutrition with a daily bowl of dirty rice. Yes, customers can be exasperating, but the fact that the store is busy probably means his grouchy ass will keep having a place to go to every day. Yes, it's a drag to get a baby shoved at you when you walk in the door, but there are people spending tens of thousands of dollars on fertilization methods or adoptions just for the opportunity to have a baby shoved at them when they walk in the door. No, it's not easy to navigate an intimate relationship with an exhausted and harried mama, but there is no shortage of people who would do anything to come home to someone named Jessica if they could.

The longer this guy remains in a low-frequency place, the more he's going to attract low-frequency occurrences. He's living in the opposite world from that other person we all know — the one who is always posting on Facebook about her new car, new lover, free tickets to Bonnaroo someone mysteriously gave her, and the cool leather jacket she just found.

I will never believe that the difference between these two comes down to luck. Each one is creating their own life from the thoughts they are continually focusing on. I learned something else recently about gratitude: When you are attuned to it, it shows up in the strangest situations. Mostly, the kinds of situations that might have gone unnoticed in the past.

A few months back, I had a moment when I felt the deepest gratitude I think I have ever felt, and what made it so incredible was that there was nothing especially earth-shattering about what was happening. My landlord walked up to my car when I was taking my two little ones to the children's museum. They were in the back seat arguing over the one American Girl doll they'd brought with them. My landlord confided in me about my next-door neighbor, who hadn't been paying her rent, and was most likely getting ready to do the midnight move.

This whole scene included different moving parts that reminded me how fortunate I am to be in recovery and living the life I decided to create for myself.

First of all, I have spent the majority of my life avoiding landlords. It didn't matter if it was my landlord or your landlord; there was a good chance I owed them money, and I avoided them like they were cops. Now, I don't even have to avoid cops.

Then there's the fact that I have two healthy little girls in the back seat arguing over an American Girl doll, not something I picked up for them at Dollar General as an afterthought.

These are all true blessings. I would not have the capacity to be a father to and care for two little girls if I was still using, and I absolutely would not be able to be present, either. When I was "out-there," my thoughts were completely occupied with how I was going to get shit, where I was going to get shit, how long until I ran out of shit, and when I'd need to get more shit. Maybe that's why people used to refer to me as a "shithead."

After talking to my landlord, I spiraled out into an endless gratitude cycle. I was in a new Toyota RAV4 — one more thing to celebrate. A few weeks earlier, I was headed over the mountain to a Sunday-afternoon gig in my Subaru when my ears were unexpectedly assaulted with the dreaded clickety-clack sound of my engine seizing. In the not-so-distant past, this would have been a long, drawn-out tragedy — but not these days. The venue owner who booked me for the gig drove out and picked me up and then, after the gig, lent me his car to drive home. On my way to his place to return the car, I stopped at the dealer with $1,000, picked out the RAV4, and signed all the paperwork like I was buying a bag of Skittles from 7-Eleven.

Think about it: (a) someone was paying me to play music in the first place; (b) he liked me so much, he lent me his car when I was in trouble; (c) I even had $1,000 cash in my drawer at home. It's all really mind-blowing.

All this gratitude springs from that one random scene in my driveway. If you sit quietly for a moment and think about it, there might be plenty for you to feel grateful for. Perhaps you should take a moment, right now, and feel the gratitude as deeply as you can.

If you are rolling your eyes, I get it. I am not Saint William. I will admit to you right now that when I leave this desk in a few minutes and head over to work, I will use the *F* word about sixteen times before I even punch the clock — I have no qualms about admitting I'm human.

I'll probably be assigned a nasty, old cigarette-smelling truck with no radio, and be sent to deliver freight in a part of New York that doesn't feel very conducive to driving a full-size tractor trailer. I have a secret weapon, though. After I get finished cursing and bitching, I breathe. I choose something happy to listen to with my Bluetooth speakers and I face the day knowing in the deepest recesses of my heart that as long as none of these things kill me, they will make me stronger.

I realize there are some people who will argue up and down — all day long — that no, everything *doesn't* happen for a reason. Sometimes things just suck and that's the way it is.

I will never believe that. Not only that, but I have a really hard time understanding what good could possibly come out of believing that. When we are faced with looking at things as either *glass half-full* or *glass half-empty*, what makes more sense? Given that what we focus on is what we get more of, the answer seems pretty obvious.

Gratitude Can Save Your Life

The idea of projecting a positive vibe is not just a goody-goody way of going through life. I'm not trying to alarm you, but I have seen firsthand how a lack of gratitude led to someone losing their life. This was a man I knew and cared for very deeply. I showed up one night at one of my favorite meetings, and he was chosen to share his story with the group (what 12 steppers refer to as *qualify*) because he had just gotten his ninety-day key tag. During the qualification, he explained how, a few months before, he had stopped doing service, stopped attending meetings, stopped calling his sponsor, and, finally, after ten years of sobriety, relapsed.

Think about the progression that led to the relapse. A definite lack of gratitude existed there. The only time a person will stop doing all the crucial steps to keep themselves safe is when they stop appreciating how important and lifesaving the steps are. They are no longer grateful for the freedom those things have given them.

I could hear it in his voice when we went out for coffee after the meeting. He was saying everything he thought I wanted to hear, but there was an emptiness inside him that I could feel viscerally. He was being swallowed up by a bad set of circumstances and allowing those circumstances to control his life. Something in my gut was telling me it wasn't going to end well for him.

This kind of thing happens all the time. Someone suffers a romantic breakup, and the reality of their partner moving on to someone else makes the idea of getting high really tempting. The pain is so great that a person might begin to tell themselves they don't care if they die. Unfortunately, with the drugs we have going around these days, that becomes a self-fulfilling prophecy.

It was really sad when I had to come to terms with the fact that this friend, whom I was sitting face-to-face with months earlier, finally overdosed and died. It was the same story you read about every day: a hot bag laced with fentanyl. The cliché "Grateful addicts don't use" used to just go through me as a weightless platitude I heard from time to time in meetings. Now it strikes me in a much different way. Now I think of my friend who lost touch with gratitude and is no longer with us as a result.

Gratitude in Advance

In addition to gratitude helping to keep us existing in a high-frequency state, receiving all the good life has to offer and assisting in the process of avoiding jails, institutions, and death, it can also help us achieve our wildest dreams.

When I was deep in the process of breaking on through to the other side — that is to say, trying to get an agent and a book deal — I was working with a life coach and learning how to set intentions and manifest those intentions by practicing what I call "gratitude in advance."

It all began innocently enough. First, I realized in the dead of winter when gigs were not very plentiful that I needed to try to raise an extra $200 a week for the next month. So I set an intention. If you've never done this, it requires many of the steps we have spoken about thus far. We make a decision to do something, we take a definite action, and we have faith that it will come to pass.

Part of the last step — the faith process — included my being thankful for, in this particular case, the extra $200 per week that I manifested. Yes, you heard me right. I was grateful for something *before* I received it. Hence the expression *gratitude in advance*. I am telling you this story because, of course,

I did wind up manifesting that $200 per week for that entire month. And then I used gratitude in advance to manifest a fancy New York City literary agent. And then, finally, a book deal.

You can do the same thing. If there's something you want to set an intention for, the steps are fairly simple: decide that you are going to get the thing, take an action toward its attainment, and begin to burst at the seams with gratitude in the all-knowing certainty that it is on its way to you. Before you know it, it will arrive.

Don't Forget about Faith

One word of caution, though. The slightest bit of skepticism will create obstacles that are utterly unnecessary. Faith means total belief. It's not considered true faith when we approach a thing with an attitude of "Let's see if this crap works." Faith means "I know this is going to work, and thank you for bringing this thing into my life."

Faith is that thing inside us that helps us do things like drive to a friend's house on a two-lane county road at night. Nobody ever gets in the car and thinks, *Well, let's see if I can get to Joe's house without someone crossing over the double yellow line, hitting me head-on, and killing and/or maiming me.* No, we get in the car knowing deep in our hearts that we are going to get there and get home safe and sound. Is there a possibility that a three-thousand-pound metal-and-glass projectile can cross an itsy-bitsy yellow line and kill us? Of course. Do we spend a lot of time thinking about that possibility? Not if we want to ever do anything.

I have several exercises I use to make gratitude an everyday action step:

1. If you've been to any 12-step meetings in your life, you've probably heard about gratitude lists. I'll be honest with you: it always used to sound like a chore to me, too. Allow me, however, to bring up a few points I once overlooked, because if you're anything like me, which by now I assume you are, you've probably overlooked them as well. Studies have demonstrated that people who regularly keep a gratitude journal just seem to enjoy their lives more. This has been proved in a quantifiable way. They sleep better and eat healthier and tend to exercise more. My assumption is that they take better care of themselves because the daily maintenance of a gratitude journal makes them appreciate life much more than in their prejournaling days. Because of this, they do everything they can to stick around longer. The trick to making it worthwhile and compelling is to do everything in your power to prevent it from *becoming* a boring chore.

    Here's what I have been doing: instead of writing that I am thankful for my three-year-old daughter, River — which just sounds flat and uninspiring — I write a detailed description of what it feels like when I take her out of her car seat and put her down and she reaches her arms up to the sky, which is the universal signal for "pick me up, Daddy." No matter how tired I am, I cannot walk past the old "arms in the sky" thing. It's beautiful, and it makes me so grateful that I am alive, that I am in recovery, and that I am present for this small child. That should give you an idea of how to keep your journal fresh and exciting.

Now, of course, you may not have a three-year-old daughter, but that certainly doesn't mean you can't do this sort of thing in your own life.

Let's say things are looking pretty bleak for you right now, but there is a glimmer of hope you're holding on to. Find one thing that makes you excited to be alive right now. Maybe it's just that you don't, at this very second, have a blaring tooth abscess. Go ahead and describe in detail the very wonderful feeling of *not* being in a state of torturous pain. If that sounds a little silly, just remember how thrilled you would be if five minutes ago you were experiencing that agony and someone came by with a magic wand and waved it at you, and that pain disappeared. It's all obviously a mindset.

If you're still having trouble, it's always helpful to think in terms of subtraction. What if certain people were no longer in your life? What if you didn't have a warm place to sleep tonight or food to eat? Or a meeting to go to when you felt the need to connect with others? Sometimes it's easier to focus on the things we take for granted if we imagine that at some point they may no longer be there.

2. This is what I call the "That Was Really Cool" exercise. Only moments ago, as I was getting ready to drop my girls back off at home, their mother texted me and asked if I could pick up a bag of ice at the gas station. I was only a minute from her house, but something told me to just do the good thing and turn around. As I walked into the gas station, I ran into a friend, who gave me a big

hug right in the doorway, and — I'll be honest — I really needed that hug at that moment. It made me feel loved, and it's the kind of connection I have been without for a little bit. Something like this is great to write about in your gratitude journal. It doesn't even really have to be that significant. Did your husband bring you a cup of coffee? Did your kid clean the snow off your car? Did a stranger stop to hold a door open or even just acknowledge you with a pleasant smile? If you can remember someone doing something nice for you recently, don't just breeze by it with the thought *That was nice. I appreciated that.* Really imagine what went through the person's mind that made them stop whatever they were doing to do something for you. Why do you think they went to the trouble? How does it make you feel to know you are so deeply cared for?

3. Whether you have an Android or an iPhone, I know there's a function where you can set an alarm to go off at the same exact time every single day. I choose 5 PM because that is usually the time I feel most stressed. Every day at that time, a bell rings and the word *Gratitude* appears on my screen. All I have to do is take a minute and envision something I am grateful for. Most of the time it is associated with something that would not exist if I weren't clean — like my children, my job, or the money in my pocket.

4. Once a week, I take an hour out of my schedule to visit with someone who helped me get to where I am right now. Sometimes it's my NA sponsor.

One time, it was this beautiful woman I didn't know from Adam who saw me playing live, introduced herself, and got me booked at the restaurant she worked at. Or sometimes I just show up at a meeting and thank everyone for helping me get my shit together. Does that mean I go around the room shaking hands and hugging people effusively? Not usually. What it usually means is that I pay it forward by keeping my eyes peeled for some dude who looks unsure of himself or out of place, and I introduce myself and give him my number. By the way, I am a guy, of course, so I make sure I only do this for another guy. Fifteen years ago, I was not so exclusive, and I kept my eyes peeled for women also. This led to a terrible relapse, so I would recommend sticking with the gender that doesn't cause your heart to go pitter-patter. Reaching out to the newcomer is the best thing we in recovery can do, and it keeps me grateful from week to week.

5. A few times a month, I get myself out on the Hudson Valley Rail Trail and take a gratitude walk. Some refer to this as a walking meditation, but it doesn't really matter what you call it, so long as you do it. As you walk, reflect on what you are grateful for. The last time I did this, it was freezing, but I spent the entire time focusing on how nice it was going to be to get back to my place and have a hot cup of tea. I then allowed myself to feel the full force of my gratitude for having a cool little apartment and the means to pay for it without a

lot of worry. From there I just kept expanding my gratitude.

You will find, as you get more adept at following these rituals, that your whole persona will attract more and more goodness into your life. This will inevitably lead to more abundance and more to be grateful for.

PART
3

KICK ASS

CHAPTER NINE

Create an Environment of Success

I f you've been fortunate enough to be pregnant or in a relationship with a pregnant woman, then you most likely understand the phenomenon of "nesting." You find out a kid is on the way and, minutes later, dust bunnies that have been living peacefully under the couch for years are suddenly, unceremoniously evicted. Or you find yourself in Home Depot looking at things called *window treatments*, and your bookshelves go from looking like a Turkish bazaar to the periodical section of the Library of Congress, all in one day.

It's a crazy instinct, but it isn't just a thing humans go through. Dogs, cats, rodents, and even honeybees experience the same thing.

I'm not going to explain in depth the evolutionary imperatives for nesting, but suffice it to say, the instinct came from a need to protect the expected infant more than to make the place look a little nicer. The fact that you just bought window treatments was, more or less, a side effect of something much more important — survival instinct.

The same can be said about this great new life you are beginning to build for yourself.

It, too, is new and fragile, and it needs to be protected and cared for that way. I'll guide you through a nesting process for that life because, as the metaphor goes, it's your "baby" and it needs protection.

So here are some questions to answer right now:

1. How does your apartment or house look? Is the paint job still fresh? Are there holes in the walls or ceilings? Are there science projects growing in your refrigerator? Are there inspiring things to look at every day? Are vision boards displayed where you can see them all the time? Does it feel like your new success is right around the corner?

   If not, you know what to do. Buy a little paint and a little spackle, and get to work. In chapter 4, I spoke about how I created a small side business in my college town, helping people prep their apartments for moving and, more importantly, get their security deposits back. It struck me as strange that people would wait until they were leaving a place before they made it look habitable. Wouldn't it be great to have a place to come home to after work that looked that nice? It really doesn't take all that much time, and it will put you in the exact mind frame you need in order to create the life I know you want.

   So, get rid of the clutter! Books you've read and don't plan on reading again, clothes you don't wear, old torn-up magazines, and broken laptops from 2003 — give 'em the heave-ho! We think more clearly when we're not surrounded by excess possessions.

2. Now that you've thrown away some books, is it time to buy more?

I'm serious. Stock your shelves with the following books (buy them used for a good price): *Awaken the Giant Within* by Anthony Robbins, *You Are a Badass at Making Money* by Jen Sincero, *Think and Grow Rich* by Napoleon Hill, *Recovery* by Russell Brand, and *The Power of Intention* by Dr. Wayne Dyer. I am not saying you have to read them all at once, but if they occupy space in your house, you may have an occasion to pick one up to read, and your life may change significantly.

3. If you own a car, how does that look?

As I said about your house, these things affect your overall headspace. If you get in your car every morning and find White Castle bags with old French fries from 2014 on the floor and junk mail in the passenger seat, and it hasn't been washed since the day *before* you had that White Castle in 2014, you should remedy that. This doesn't necessarily mean spending $150 at a car detailer, either. Consider spending an hour on a Saturday to spruce up ol' Bertha.

Having a clean car to drive, in addition to a clean house to come home to, will make a vast difference in your ability to think and plan. Human beings are extraordinarily emotional creatures, and we tend to be affected greatly by the look and feel of our surroundings. This is a time-tested truth. Look at the famous daily to-do list of Benjamin Franklin, and you will see that one of the most prominent entries on the list was to "put things in their places" at the end of each day. This was the guy who was responsible for the invention of the bifocal lens, the rocking chair, *Poor Richard's Almanack*, and our present understanding of electricity. I bet he couldn't have done all those things with old snuffboxes and torn-up waistcoats lying around. Or so he believed. Who are we to argue, though? If it was good enough for Benji, it's good enough for us.

Your Relationship with Money: It's Complicated

Now that you've taken care of your house and car, your lovely little habitats for the creation and growth of your new and exciting life, we should take a look at your inherent attitudes about money. I have found through research and personal experience that money is one of the most emotionally charged areas for a majority of people. As a matter of fact, there is usually quite a bit of confusion among people regarding their attitudes about it and their behaviors with it. Before I turned my life around, my relationship with money was deplorable. Like many others in active addiction, often money would be owed before it was even earned.

For a person who has never struggled with addiction, the idea of going through old journals and bumping into a fifteen-year-old suicide note is, most likely, a foreign one — but for those of us on *this* planet, I can't imagine I'm the only one. Many of us reached this point before we sought help. When I found my suicide note from way back in 2003, it really drove home how much things have changed for me.

It was about five or six months after my first kid's mother took our then-three-year-old daughter and moved back to

Staten Island, about two hours away. For the first few months, I kind of ignored what was going on. Or I may have been in denial. Either way, my initial reaction to her leaving was relief. I was happy to be alone. When it sunk in a few months later that I was no longer going to be in my daughter's life, that her mother was going to start dating other men, and that my life was never going to be the same again, I began my first serious trip to *rock bottom.*

This being my first journey of this kind, it turned out to be a very long and horrible one. I had never been exposed to recovery. I had never gone to a detox, never set foot inside a drug rehab, and never been to a 12-step meeting. As far as I was concerned at that point, I never would. The whole thing seems ludicrous to me now, but without any frame of reference, all those options didn't seem to me like…well, options.

The only answer I could think of was to leave our apartment in the Hudson Valley and move back to my mother's house. This was an ill-advised move because she had prescriptions for a hundred different things, and I wasn't there for longer than a week before I started stealing everything she had. A morphine pill here. A Valium there. A couple of Dilaudid.

She kicked me out within the span of two weeks.

My health, as you might expect, was in a terrible condition. My gut was bloated and swollen from the constant use of opioids and the less-than-constant use of the bathroom. I spent the average day swinging on a pendulum from nodding out to dope sick to depression to mania. I was missing two or three front teeth. It was one of the worst periods of my life.

I was what is commonly referred to in recovery parlance as "sick and suffering." Physically, emotionally, and spiritually. More spiritually than anything else. None of that reality was any good, but the fact that I was missing front teeth was the one aspect that kept making me wake up every morning wishing I was dead. Eventually, I went from the wishing stage to the planning stage.

Most of it was rooted in ego. I knew that my ex was dating someone else. She mentioned to me that he was twelve years younger than I was, so of course, I allowed that imagery to take me to the darkest hell I could possibly imagine. As I said, I was spiritually sick.

All of this came flooding back when I found that note. It was as if I was right back there again for a minute, and when I returned to present-day reality, it gave me the biggest chill down my spine.

It was going to cost me $1,500 to get my teeth fixed, and the possibility of getting my hands on that kind of money, at that time, was close to nil. I know this because it's all right there in the note.

I'm making this point because when I was finally introduced to NA a few weeks after I wrote that note, my life took a 180-degree turn. I met other addicts who took me under their wing and loved me instantly and unconditionally. My health began to improve greatly. And I was finally able to save the $1,500 I needed to take care of my smile.

Being able to do that for myself was no small feat. It was one of my first lessons about money and financial abundance. Like a lot of the things we've discussed thus far, what I was telling myself when I hit bottom was my reality. As long as I was buying into the fact that $1,500 was out of reach, it was.

Now it's a drop in the bucket. I'm not trying to impress you or anything, but during weeks when I am booked to play gigs on Saturday and Sunday, I can clear close to that when combined with my paycheck. I am mentioning this because I believe, in my heart, that you and I are the same in many ways.

If I switched things up and got where I am, you have every reason to believe you can do the same!

First, though, you need to check your deepest attitudes when it comes to money. I use the word "deepest" because many of us believe that, yes, we'd love to have plenty of money. I mean, who wouldn't? But if we dig a little deeper, we find we've been indoctrinated with some of the strangest drivel regarding money, and it affects us by getting in the way of our having any.

Expressions we've heard all our lives — such as "Money is the root of all evil," "Money isn't everything," "Money can't buy happiness," and "The best things in life are free" — tend to get wrapped up in our subconscious thoughts and confuse us. The confusion comes from the fact that, in reality, we need money to survive, and since we have gone through all the trouble of putting down our addictions and making a better life for ourselves, survival is the low rung on the ladder. We don't want to just survive. We want to thrive. Thriving takes an abundance of money.

So, before we can take care of the actual mechanics behind making an abundance of money, we need to address our confusing relationship with it.

Mary's Dilemma

Let me give you a perfect example: there's a woman we'll call Mary whom I've had the luxury of observing for the last twenty-five years. One of my first memories of her, when we were kids away at college, was hearing her on a pay phone (texting hadn't been invented yet) shaking her dad down for cash. This was usually followed by a three-day vigil she held by the mailbox as she waited for the money to arrive.

Now, years later, anytime I am on the phone with Mary

and I tell her about something positive that happened to me, she finds a way to direct the conversation to how poorly she's doing, and how a little money could surely help her. It reached a point where I just stopped calling her. Not that I resented giving her the money, but for someone who has said, "I hate money," a hundred times over the years, she certainly doesn't have much time to think of anything else. Do you see the paradox? When someone "hates" a thing and is simultaneously consumed by the thought of it, they make for terrible company.

But there's more to it than that. Mary is a person who has demonstrated what is known as a *scarcity mindset*. She has always believed, both consciously and subconsciously, that she has never had enough money. And because of this, it will always be true. Am I saying that a person should tell themselves they're rich even if they're not? Well, sort of.

As I mentioned in the chapter before this one, *if you do not live in a place of gratitude, you will never have anything to be grateful for.*

Even I have a little debt going on. It's difficult not to. I don't focus on that, though. I stay in a place of gratitude for all the things I do have, and I keep my reticular activating system homed in on where the money is, and it all seems to work out.

Obsessing about debt is really the last thing you should do. When a person wakes up every morning with their first thought attached to their debt and the worry that accompanies it, they tend to accrue more debt and almost become paralyzed by it. I, of course, would never suggest ignoring it, but making it your sole focus is toxic.

The Only Way Out Is Through

If you have a lot of debt and it seems to overwhelm you, there's really only one way to handle it — head-on. As I said, ignoring it is dangerous, and obsessing over it is poisonous. What you need to do is open your notebook and make an accounting page of everything you owe. What's good about this is that it will all be right out in the open, you won't be hiding from it, and now you can begin to plan how you will dig yourself out.

The first thing that will help is increasing your income, obviously. Back in my days as a $350-per-week cab driver, the idea of paying down debt seemed about as viable as opening for Kanye at Madison Square Garden. I ate a lot of peanut butter and jelly back then. One of the best things about the fact that I am now in the "$1,000-a-week take-home" club is that paying off a $500 debt in a month's time can be done without affecting my diet all that much.

Let us say, for argument's sake, though, that there you are looking at your notebook and you owe $6,000 in credit-card debt, you have a $1,500 tax lien for a 1099 you just happened to forget to declare as income on your taxes last year, and you're on the hook for a $2,700 loan for a car that stopped running three months ago. That's a little over ten grand. Now you take into account that you are making $25,000 a year. It'd be easy to throw your hands in the air, admit defeat, and look for something to binge-watch on Netflix.

Or, you could realize that $10,000 is a little less than $200 a week for a year.

This "insurmountable" debt now begins to look a lot more manageable. Make the hard-core decision to crawl out from the wreckage and, as we have discussed on numerous occasions throughout this book, take an action step toward that decision. Jump and the net will appear.

The thing I learned in my journey is that money is an energy. It is a tool of exchange. Think about it: Can you honestly say that $50 someone makes in a crack deal is the same as

$50 someone makes by selling one of their paintings? Hardly. This is why it is so important to cultivate a loving relationship with money. If you learn to love it, it will love you, but if you "hate money" the way Mary does, you will always be running after it the way she is.

If you are thinking, *Okay, Billy, you were fine for most of this book, but now you are getting out of hand. People who love money are shallow and superficial, and I am a lot deeper than that*, I get where you are coming from, but hear me out.

The most spiritual I have ever been in my life is when I got to a point where I could reach out to a friend who was struggling financially and offer to help, or when I was able to pay for child support and daycare. On time. Every week. Or when I became a father who was engaged with my children and not off having an anxiety attack about not being able to cover the bills.

The philosophy of broke people being the most spiritual is a lie perpetuated by those who try to justify their own poverty by misinterpreting the same phrases that have been misinterpreted for hundreds, if not thousands, of years.

The Bible quote that people like to bring up, "Money is the root of all evil," is not even the actual quote. The verse from 1 Timothy 6:10 is "For the love of money is the root of all evil." That's a big difference. The quote refers to people who deify and worship money. I mean, sure, we can all agree that those kinds of people are lame. But the point is that money, all by itself, is not evil. It's just a tool to help you buy toilet paper.

That other quote, "It's easier for a camel to get through the eye of a needle than it is for a rich man to get to heaven," is another common bastardization. The real quote is "How hard it is for the rich to enter the kingdom of God! Indeed, it is easier for a camel to go through the eye of a needle than for someone who is rich to enter the kingdom of God!" If you were to continue reading in the Book of Luke where this quote originates, you would see that what Jesus was trying to explain was that no one can buy their way into heaven. It is only through grace that someone enters. This goes for both the rich man and the poor man.

People throughout history have misinterpreted the Bible to justify everything from hating on the gay community to making life miserable for women. It's all bullshit, and the poverty mindset is no exception. The truth of the matter is that where there is money, there is better health. There is freedom. There are options. Where there is lack and scarcity, there is usually crime. People are forced into lives they don't want to live. There is domestic violence and child neglect. There is prostitution. There is addiction and people dying from overdose.

Of course, these tragedies exist in wealthy communities, also, but those are usually anomalies. It's more the exception than the rule. In poverty-stricken areas, this goes on every day, en masse. You don't need to be a star statistician to recognize that three of America's poorest regions — West Virginia, New Mexico, and the District of Columbia — are also in the top ten for the most drug-related deaths. I challenge anyone to find anything spiritual about those facts.

The idea that wealthy people can be shady is true. There will always be wealthy people who take advantage of others; but I don't have to tell you, if you've ever been sold any beat drugs or ghosted by someone who went to cop for you, there are plenty of poor people that take advantage of others, also. At the same time, there will always be rich people who care deeply for others, just as there are poor people who care deeply for others. There is no across-the-board truth about these things.

The best thing you can do for yourself and for everyone around you is to become the biggest, baddest version of yourself that you can possibly create. When you are a living example of playing big, you give the people around you permission to become just as big. It is practically your responsibility to push yourself to the limit. This includes your relationship with money and the vision you have for yourself.

Here are a few exercises to get your money game on track.

1. Open your notebook and write a letter to money. You heard me right. Forget about how stupid you think this exercise is. I'm going to guess that this is not the first exercise in this book you have found preposterous, so why stop now? Seriously, write a stream-of-consciousness letter to money. It might start out something like this:

   Dear Money,
   I love when I have enough of you to get the things I need to survive, to pay my electric bill, and to fill my house with groceries, but you piss me off when I get hit with a car-insurance bill I wasn't expecting and there's just not enough of you to go around. It stresses me out.

   Just let 'er rip. It's incredibly important to know where you stand with your attitudes about money, and this little exercise will be a real eye-opener.

2. Think of a time when money came to you unexpectedly. Write a brief description of that time. How did it make you feel? What did you use the money for? Do you think it is possible for something like this to happen again?

3. What do you plan to do the next time an unexpected financial windfall shows up? This paragraph will work the most magic if you really get detailed with it. Try to go beyond just wishing and hoping and dreaming. Put yourself in a place where a few thousand dollars that you weren't expecting just show up out of the blue. What are some things you'd do with the cash? Take your sweetie to dinner? Pay something off?

Finally, take my advice. If at all possible, keep a couple hundred dollars on you at all times. If that isn't possible, keep a roll of forty singles and a ten-dollar bill in your pocket. If you don't have fifty dollars, figure out how to get it. Legally. It will remind you, on many different levels, that money is always available and always within your reach. Walking around penniless sends the wrong signal to your psyche.

Keep a little hidden in your house, too — once again, it's the signal you are sending to your brain consciously and unconsciously. When you believe, in your heart of hearts, that money is always around you, you will soon find that it is true. You are the executive producer of your life on this planet. Act accordingly.

CHAPTER TEN

Prepare for Takeoff

As you are driving (or walking, crawling, or sometimes hobbling) down the road to achieving greatness, there will be certain pitfalls along the way that may seem like they're trying to pull the proverbial rug out from under you.

A few years ago, I was do-do-doing through life when I became the victim of some of the most annoying bullshit you could imagine. I was in line at the supermarket with about thirty dollars' worth of groceries, when the cashier summarily informed me my debit card was declined. I knew it had to be some kind of mistake, because I had gotten paid three days before and, last time I checked, I had six or seven hundred dollars in the account.

"Sorry," she said. "It keeps saying 'declined.'"

Luckily, I had a little cash on me. When the checkout-line nightmare was over, I packed the groceries and the kids in the car, and we stopped at the bank to do some quick investigating.

I was told that some law firm I had never heard of had a judgment against me, and froze my checking account. The bank teller explained that all she could do was give me their name and phone number.

I was honestly perplexed. Puzzled. Pissed off.

I called my sponsor. After three years in recovery, this was what I had been programmed to do when the shit hit the fan. I'm sure you can relate. A sponsor, we are told from practically our first day in any 12-step program, is there to offer their experience, strength, and hope. In this particular case, my sponsor had the strength and hope, but — never having had a law firm pillage his checking account — he was short on experience. That's okay. He talked me down off the ledge, so to speak, and advised me to call the law firm immediately.

It turned out they were a special kind of law firm. They were not the sort of law firm that helps victims of domestic violence. They were not the kind that assists industrial accident victims in getting compensated for loss of wages. In fact, they were not helping anyone but themselves. This particular law firm goes to credit-card companies and "buys" what is commonly referred to as "bad debt." In other words, they buy lists of names — of people who defaulted on their debt with a credit-card company, the amount of debt they defaulted on, and their last known address. They take a debt of, say, $1,200, which they pay about $65 for, add on $4,500 in "legal and administrative fees," and then sue you *in absentia* for the money. As in, you're not there and not informed. Soon after this, they receive a judgment in their favor, and they go about the business of finding your checking account — sometimes years later — and freezing your funds. This is how they get your attention.

Of course, they didn't tell me any of this. I found out most of my information from a Google search. I called the law firm, was screened by what sounded like a call center overseas, and was then transferred to a Mr. Lewis, ostensibly at the law firm.

"Mr. Manas, we are looking to collect on a Parliament Bank credit card you defaulted on," he said.

"Parliament Bank? You mean from 1999?" I asked.

"It doesn't matter how long ago it was. You still owe the money. This kind of thing will ruin your credit rating, you know. Now, I may be able to help you work out a payment plan, but I will have to run it by my supervisor. How much of a down payment are you able to come up with?"

A blog article I read online mentioned that I should ask them to mail me a copy of the judgment and all legal paperwork pertaining to the case, so I did just that. Truthfully, it felt empowering to not just roll over and start working out a payment plan with this schlub.

"I will send you a copy of the judgment, Mr. Manas, but really it'd be in your best interest to get this thing squared away as soon as possible so it doesn't destroy your credit."

"I'd appreciate it if you'd stop trying to threaten me and just send the paperwork."

On and on — the call continued like that for close to twenty-five minutes.

What I am about to explain to you might be valuable if you ever find yourself in the same position.

I am all for being a responsible adult and paying my debts. That is a large part of my recovery and making my prescribed steps toward my goals. The idea of becoming a debt-free person who doesn't cringe when a bill comes in the mail seemed impossible to me at one time. But as I've described, carrying out a plan I put in place helped me to become that person.

In this case, however, we were talking about a fifteen-year-old debt that had been "bought" for pennies on the dollar, and inflated to almost five times its original size by a predatory litigation factory. The gloves were, shall we say, off.

(By the way, I've learned to detect when it's worth taking my gloves off, and when it's not. You will, too, after you learn which of your battles are or are not worth fighting. Always take note of this so you can grow. Learn from the times you go too far, or not far enough. Be ready to think through the big picture when a situation like the one I'm describing drops in to rattle your cage.)

The first thing I noticed in the law firm's paperwork was that they received a default judgment from a court in Staten Island. I had been working and living in Ulster County, New York, at the time, and I knew I could find proof of that somewhere. This was good. All I needed to do was call that court, ask for a date, and fight the judgment on the grounds that they had the wrong address on the court notice. That was enough to have the judgment vacated. If you find yourself in a similar situation, you can do the exact same thing. Different states have different laws, but for the most part, if you can prove that you never had a chance to defend yourself, a judge has to vacate the judgment.

This is not as difficult as it might sound. I learned through this process that a very simple explanation of never having gotten a court notice will usually suffice.

That doesn't necessarily mean your troubles are over, though. It just means that you've turned the clocks back to before you had the judgment, and now you need to defend yourself.

So, generally, to do this, you need to show up for a second court date.

And make sure you know your rights. When I went to court after I had my judgment vacated, I witnessed dozens of unsuspecting people, most obviously first-generation immigrants, in the same situation as I was, negotiating with attorneys for payment plans and all kinds of heinous outcomes that were utterly unnecessary.

Unfortunately, these kinds of predatory companies get extraordinarily wealthy by betting that most people don't know better. Now is your chance to not be one of those people. The truth of the matter is, unless the law firm can show documentation to verify your original debt (in this case it was $1,200 from 1999), they are not legally entitled to collect any portion of it. They are certainly not allowed to charge you any interest or fees on it, either.

So, after hours of sitting in that courtroom at my second court date, an attorney for the predators came over to try the same ruse on me that she'd succeeded in using with everyone else.

"Look," she said in her hurried tone, "if you are having trouble paying your debt, I understand. I've worked out some payment plans with some other folks today; maybe I can help you get your debt paid down in small installments."

"No," I replied.

"No?" she repeated.

"I'd like to go in front of the judge."

"Suit yourself," she said indignantly.

A few minutes later, I was called up to the bench, and the judge asked me how I planned to pay my debt. I replied that I didn't remember any such debt, and I would like to see documentation supporting their allegations. In other words, unless this law firm could produce a receipt for the cheeseburger I charged in 1999, they were out of luck, and they knew it.

The fact that I knew it, too, was new ground for me.

As I mentioned, these predatory companies buy lists of names with amounts owed and addresses on them. They do not have the time or space to store supporting documentation on these debts. Their lawyers could tell immediately that I knew how the law worked so they quietly asked the judge to discharge the case. Every single person in that court on that day could have done the same exact thing, but they did not know any better. So, the attorney got rid of me quickly so she could shake down the dozens of others who were left waiting. As far as she was concerned, I was a cancer, and it was highly probable that I could infect the rest of her profits unless I was cut out immediately.

I got in my car that cold February afternoon and in my head played back the tape of everything that had just happened — from that uncomfortable situation in the grocery store to the present.

I felt a fundamental shift had taken place in my life. The only thing that felt better than knowing that I just challenged "the man" and won was when that $600 was released back into my checking account a few days later.

Once again, the precedent effect was in full swing. I no longer felt like a hapless victim in a cruel world. I felt like I had some control over my own life. I didn't realize it at the time, but of the very many things that changed for me while I was in recovery, my approach to life situations in general was likely the most important. But it didn't just happen by itself. It came as the result of certain moves I had made years earlier.

In a case such as this one, my usual attitude had been to spin off into a dark corner, obsessing about how unjust the world was and how the big guy was always exploiting the little guy. If I used my old approach, I'd get my old result — meaning I'd be a victim.

I had gone through a change since I had gotten sober, and it was a lot more than just not using substances.

It involved learning to reclaim my own power to affect situations in my life.

Constant and Never-Ending Improvement

Sometime around 2013, I picked up my first Anthony Robbins book, and I became completely hooked on the idea that my life could improve well beyond anything I had ever imagined. I'd found one of his audio programs while I was at the height of my active addiction, and even though I knew his theories and principles were all sound, I was in no condition, at that time, to make use of them.

When I was introduced to him again, with over three years of sustained recovery, I knew the time was right for me to employ the information. Recovery gives you that kind of insight, by the way.

Much of what Tony Robbins teaches is based on the Japanese philosophy of *kaizen*. This means to improve a little bit every single day. Robbins decided that we needed an American phrase that meant the same thing and developed what he called CANI. This is an acronym for *constant and never-ending improvement*. This may sound trite and flat, but consider it for a second. A lot of us want enormous, monumental change in our lives but give up quickly because we get scared of the enormous, monumental amount of work it might take to accomplish the change.

This is not the case at all.

Once you understand, on a visceral level, that massive change requires only daily incremental action, it suddenly becomes a lot more realistic.

I fell in love with these ideas, and I wanted to immerse myself in as much information as possible. Once I read and listened to everything I could find from Tony Robbins, I went looking for more motivation and guidance, anywhere I could find it. I read Zig Ziglar, Jim Rohn, Napoleon Hill, Jen Sincero, Dr. Wayne Dyer — the list of available help is virtually endless.

In the past, my habit was to get super excited about something to the point where I'd be completely obsessed and think about nothing else. For about a week. I did this when I started working out with weights, when I decided I was going to learn everything there was to know about day-trading, when I started any Charles Dickens novel, and anytime I decided to get serious about my grades in school. Being inconsistent was the only consistent thing about me.

This obsession with self-improvement, however, changed all that for me. In a lot of the information available in the self-improvement realm, consistency is one of the crucial lessons to learn and adopt, but it goes a little deeper than that. It's one thing to read about something and understand on an intellectual level that it can help you — it's another thing entirely when you put something into action and see results from it.

It goes right back to the very primal pleasure/pain principle I discussed in chapter 2. When the results of my sticking with, and even improving upon, my self-study with motivational principles began to materialize in a tangible way — like, say, squeaking out of a bogus $5,700 debt — it brought me a lot of pleasure, and it prevented pain I would have experienced in the past. I was hooked!

I brought up the story about the predatory law firm because it best illustrates the dramatic shift that took place in my life as a result of changing my old behaviors. In the past, I would have taken the $600 loss of funds from my bank account, seen myself as a victim, told anyone who would listen about how terribly I had been treated by life, and then hid from the further pursuit of the law firm. I would have given up on having a checking account at all and joined all the other angry people in the check-cashing line, and the attorneys would have gone about the business of changing my credit score from 550 to 400.

This was Billy Manas style, from high school until age 43. That transformation is what makes me so passionate about bringing all this information to you. I am the ultimate test case. If I was able to adopt a completely different persona, you definitely can.

The Seven-Day Mental Positivity Diet

One tool responsible for the biggest change in the way I handled my life is a small pamphlet by the author Emmet Fox called "The Seven-Day Mental Diet." It was first published in 1935, so if you can locate it, you'll probably find the language to be a bit hokey. That aside, though, the principle behind it is just as valuable today as it was eighty-five years ago. I've added the word *positivity* to the name of the diet so that you can have that word uppermost in mind while you're in the midst of the challenge.

The premise is that you commit to seven days of not allowing yourself to have a negative thought. Let me rephrase that: seven days of not *dwelling* on a negative thought. One may pop into your mind, but the instructions are to brush it off as quickly as you would if a burning ember popped out of a fire onto your Diesel jeans.

If it sounds easy, let me assure you — it's not. It was so difficult, in fact, that the period is stuck in my mind to this day.

Here's what you need to consider: This means no gossiping, no road rage, no quiet judgments to yourself about the guy sitting next to you in Burger King picking his teeth — nothing. Oh, and something awful is bound to happen in that seven-day period that is going to really test your dedication. How do I know this? It says as much in the pamphlet, and it came true for me. Man, did it come true for me.

The transmission blew on my 1991 convertible Saab during my Seven-Day Mental Positivity Diet. To tell you the truth, I'm not sure I would commit to trying to go on the diet again. The good news is, it is unlike many of the other aspects of self-improvement. Most self-improvement techniques require daily maintenance, but not so with the diet. Once you get through the seven days successfully, you have so thoroughly reprogrammed your way of perceiving the world and your circumstances that it's not really necessary to do much to maintain it. The thing is, if you blow it on the third, fourth, or fifth day, you have to stop the diet immediately. The instructions are to wait a few days and start again. As I keep saying, it's not easy, but if you're able to pull it off, your life will likely never be the same.

In the situation with my car, I could not allow myself to spin off into a maelstrom of worry, fear, anger, and frustration. I actually had to follow the directions of the diet and ask myself, *What is good about this situation?*

I wanted to kick the back fender and scream "Nothing!" but I waited a second. I asked myself the question again. It was hard. I mean, yes, the car was almost twenty-five years old, but I have always adored convertibles. Every day that I drove it was fun. I knew that the old Saab and I were forced to now part ways. Sinking thousands into a new, or even a rebuilt, transmission would not be worthwhile.

The idea behind the diet is not to simply try to turn yourself into a mindless Pollyanna. No one is telling you to stand outside in the middle of a rainstorm repeating, "It's not raining. It's not raining." Instead, your mission is to get an umbrella and then spend a little time taking in the sights and sounds of a beautiful spring shower. The way the raindrops line up on a shutter and jump off one by one or the percussive sound they make as they pound onto the awnings and rooftops. Come on, do it. Think about it. There's beauty there, and the quality of your life can increase exponentially if you have the ability to see it instead of cursing about how wet you're getting. Just be prepared with that umbrella. Or know you can get one easily.

So, by the third or fourth time I asked myself that question, I began to laugh. My daughter Gloria, who was three years old at the time, *hated* that car. The idea of the roof disappearing sent her into toddler hysterics.

Well, I thought, *Gloria will be relieved.* Silver lining.

As I sat in the passenger seat waiting for the tow-truck driver to hook up my car and drive me back home, I took a second to get grateful. I thought about what a miracle it was that I had enough money in the bank so the $100 tow was not going to set me back financially. Not too long ago, it absolutely would have. Hey, I found something else good about what, at first glance, seemed like an awful situation.

As you might have guessed, I got through that challenge. I managed to not miss a single day of work, and soon I was driving something else. It turned out to be a valuable lesson for me. I could have handled that fateful Thursday two different ways, but what my life looked like on the following Tuesday would have been exactly the same. Except, perhaps, if I had allowed myself to turn into a manic bowl of quivering Jell-O, leaving myself and everyone around me worse for the wear.

If you decide to go ahead and try the Seven-Day Mental Positivity Diet, keep in mind that it is not a thing to be tackled lightly. You need to have an almost severe sense of commitment with it. Once again, it is probably one of the most difficult challenges in this entire book. The lifelong benefits will be worth it, though. You will never be able to return to your old, destructive patterns of thought again without at least some awareness of them.

I actually changed some of my language when I was on the Seven-Day Mental Positivity Diet. You may notice I rarely use the word *problem*. I learned to use the word *challenge* in its place.

When it comes to changing our lives, the way we communicate to ourselves is just as important as our physiology. Our internal language steers our thoughts, and our thoughts guide our entire lives. The benefits of changing the way we word things to ourselves are endless. What we are doing, in a sense, is reprogramming lifelong behaviors. In the 12-step programs people say, "Once you know, you cannot not know." It's the same with the "diet." Once you have experienced life for an entire week in this way, it's practically impossible to go back to how you perceived things in the past.

I truly recommend doing this for yourself. You may not realize it on a conscious level, but you might have old patterns that you run whenever things get tough. You may have a tendency to slip into guilty feelings or blame others in a subtle way for difficulties you face from day to day. It's really hard to tell just from sitting there trying to think about it. As a matter of fact, you could possibly be in denial about it. I have always considered myself to be one of the most emotionally evolved men on the planet — until I have found myself throwing a coffee cup out my window at the guy who just flipped me off at the traffic light. The mental diet aided in the task of changing these bad habits.

My run-in with the law firm took place a couple of years after my Seven-Day Mental Positivity Diet, a testament to how this sort of reprogramming works. Of course, when I initially became aware of the injustice, I was angry. So angry that I had to call my sponsor. And I'm not saying I went through those seven days and now I whistle and hum right through every tragic event in my life. I did, however, find a proactive way to correct my situation once I had a minute to stew about it. As I mentioned, I kept reminding myself that I was being faced with a challenge — not a problem. This makes a big difference.

I can assure you that I am not perfect. I'll find myself from time to time — even today — bitching to my coworkers about the boss, making fun of someone I don't particularly care for, and even getting into an unresourceful state here and there, but I brush those things off me as soon as I can.

Life is never going to be perfect. Girlfriends, boyfriends, wives, husbands, bosses, customers, the guy tailgating us even though we're driving ten miles over the speed limit — they're all put in our lives to teach us things. Sometimes those things are insights about ourselves we need to face. Sometimes it's simply the patience we so desperately need on occasion. When we are able to accept the lessons from imperfections, we gain power.

CHAPTER ELEVEN

Seal Off the Exits

After the Staten Island court case, positive events in my life progressed at a fast clip. I was granted my first post-recovery credit card — with a humble $300 credit limit, but still. My FICO score, while still embarrassingly low, was not quite as low as it had been. I was using a debit card to pay for everything in those days, so my strategy was to use my new credit card instead and pay it down immediately. With the advent of iPhone apps, paying a credit-card bill was now an instantaneous process, and before long, a $300 limit became a $1,500 limit, and two credit cards became three, then four, then six. Sometime in 2014, I logged onto one of those free-credit-score sites and there it was — the impossible dream — a 701 FICO score. This score, as some of you may already know, is the kind of score that makes a person eligible for car loans at major car dealerships, better insurance rates, and even a mortgage, should a person want to pursue that kind of thing.

I have received many gifts since my journey in the world of recovery began, but this one was of the "I have to pinch myself" variety. I kept staring at the screen thinking, *Me. Billy Manas. 701 credit score.* It gave me a feeling of legitimacy that I never thought I'd feel. I flashed back to that morning when I was hitting bottom, sitting in front of the bakery in Rosendale.

What a life-affirming journey it had all been.

Then the wheels in my lucid, "four years without a drink or a drug" brain kept turning. That 701 score was not just something nice to stare at. It was a tool, the likes of which I had never been given to work with, and I had to figure out how to use it to propel myself even further into the life of my most ambitious dreams.

Want to hear something really crazy? After busting my ass to finally achieve great credit, my next step was to max out my credit cards by getting myself an expensive life coach. Yup, I went into debt all over again. I knew how easy it would be for me to get complacent with this bit of success I had just achieved. The relapse I experienced years before was still fresh in my memory. I'm not sure I can properly convey to you how badly I did not want that to happen again. So, I left myself no other option but to succeed. Now I had help, help I was paying for, to make sure I succeeded.

When facing the decision of whether or not to go ahead with the life coach, I fell into one of those YouTube rabbit holes that we sometimes find ourselves in when we are procrastinating. I landed on an interview with Jim Carrey where he was telling a story about his father.

His father, he explained, had been just as funny as Jim was. In fact, his dad had inspired all of his son's comedic talent. The older Carrey never pursued a career in comedy because he felt like it'd be more practical to take a job as an accountant. However, he was laid off when Jim was twelve, and he never really got over it. This taught Jim something very important: that it's just as easy to fail at what you don't want to do as it is to fail at going for your dreams.

That did it for me. I made the commitment.

This was not something I took lightly. I knew if I made any false steps here, I'd once again destroy my credit. So, the possibility that I'd blow off appointments with my coach, or not follow through on the goals we set from one week to the next, was nonexistent. Not only did I know where I stood, but I felt as if I had sent a clear message to the entire world. I was not fucking around.

Hiring a life coach is not a terribly crazy proposition. I paid about $5,000 for an entire year with my first one, and I know I accomplished the things I did because she was there for me. Sometimes we brainstormed together. Sometimes she suggested strategies and sent me links to materials that helped me, and sometimes she just reminded me who I was, after those tough weeks when it seemed like the world was trying to convince me that I was nothing special.

And while all this was invaluable, the most important part was the form I filled out the day before our first appointment. It kept me accountable.

Every January 1, hundreds of thousands of people make resolutions about losing weight, putting down the cigarettes, writing a book, and even getting sober. Statistically speaking, 80 percent of them have given up by February 15. There are many reasons for this, but I believe one of the most important is the lack of accountability. When you go ahead and spend a huge chunk of cash — especially cash you can't really afford to spend on, say, a life coach — you will be a lot less apt to make excuses and a lot more likely to stick to your plans, if for no other reason than to earn back the money you owe.

The common attitude in this society is to look upon this kind of behavior as ridiculous. I cannot tell you the number of times people have side-eyed me like I was some kind of gullible sucker whenever I told them about my investment in a life coach — possibly the same people who don't blink at the prospect of borrowing $75,000 to go to a state university and come out with a degree in communications.

The humorous reality of all this is that, if you happen to be among the fortunate ones, that degree will land you a position with a $30,000-a-year starting salary. My coach, on the other hand, paid for herself with some of the business ideas and goals we dreamed up, as I plugged away at putting together my book proposal.

Don't take what I just said the wrong way. There's nothing wrong with going away to school. I certainly did it, and I consider those five years as some of the most important of my life. The late-night philosophical conversations, the bed hopping, the exposure to cultures and people I never would have experienced anywhere else — I wouldn't trade any of it. Even if I could take away the $50,000 student-loan albatross that is still hanging around my neck twenty-five years later. I'm simply making the point that it seems arbitrary that most people take student debt — which has just reached $1.5 trillion in the United States — in stride but balk at spending a few thousand dollars on a year of life coaching.

Maybe I haven't convinced you to give life coaching a shot. If so, I respect that decision — you can still put your own back against the wall without spending money you don't have or are not comfortable spending. Allow me to enumerate a few ways.

Applying Leverage

Do you have any annoying friends? That's a silly question, right? We all have annoying friends. You've most likely never realized that your most grating and obnoxious friends could be the perfect ones to tell that you have to quit smoking or start a business or leave that abusive boyfriend. Why? *Because they are going to remind you and needle you every day until you follow through.* You'll have no choice. You'll do anything to get them to shut up.

Going on Facebook and making big, bold announcements to your 1,200 friends can also add some needed pressure to your life. You'll now run into these folks at the supermarket, and they'll ask you how the nursing-school thing turned out or if you found a good truck to open your hot-dog stand with yet. The reason it's so important to either hire a life coach or tell an annoying friend — or, for that matter, a lot of annoying friends — that you are committed to making massive changes in your life is because it affords you one of the key elements of change: leverage.

A lever is a machine created to move an enormous amount of weight that you otherwise couldn't budge. If you've ever used a crowbar to pry anything open, you know what I'm talking about. Getting leverage on yourself to make a change just means the pain got so severe for you that you were moved to finally do something about it.

A perfect example is when you finally decided to start your recovery journey. As most of us know firsthand, hitting bottom — that place we get to right before we start climbing back up — is one of the most painful experiences of our lives. So painful, in fact, that if you've been to enough meetings, you'll hear people talk about how loony they start to get around their anniversary date. The memory of that enormous pain sometimes creates a certain post-traumatic stress. If you've ever been in the unenviable position of trying to talk someone "into" getting in recovery, or even going to their first meeting, you already know how stubborn and pigheaded a person can be when they're still using. Anything *less* than an event or series of events that could induce post-traumatic stress wouldn't be strong enough leverage.

But look, you don't need to know the psychological terminology to realize that, in order to live the life of your wildest dreams, you need to start by making small changes and building them up over time. It all begins by getting your ass to a meeting. Or just by not using or drinking. As you start feeling good about yourself, you want more of that feeling. You create bigger and more compelling goals for yourself. It's a wonderful, never-ending loop of positive reinforcement.

It All Comes Down to Feelings

I feel incredibly passionate about spreading information on setting and achieving goals. As soon as I figured out how to change my life so drastically, my initial response was to tell anyone and everyone, from friends and family to audiences of jail inmates.

"You can do this!" I shout from the rooftops. "Set a goal. Wake up every morning and try to do one thing that will get you closer to achieving it. Don't stop until you've pushed past the point where you feel like it'll never happen. Then, try a little harder. A little while after that, you will have achieved the goal."

When you think about why we do any of this stuff, you'll realize that it is not to have a nice car, a big house, or a hot boyfriend or girlfriend. It is the *feeling* pursuing goals gives us. No matter what it is you want, when you break it down you'll notice that the reason you want it is for the feeling you believe it's going to give you. Try it on yourself. Think about any of your dreams and consider why you want it.

Why do you want a lot of money?

"Because if I had a lot of money, I wouldn't have to work a crappy job and be bossed around by an obnoxious supervisor."

Why do you want a hot girlfriend?

"Because if I had a hot girlfriend, people would know I was someone special."

Why do you want your book to be a huge hit?

"Because I could change so many lives and help thousands of people."

Every one of those answers comes down to the feelings that those things can provide. So, we really don't want things. We want to change our feelings.

Doesn't it make sense, then, that we should try to get a handle on our feelings at the beginning of this new journey? If we don't, none of that stuff is going to make us feel what we're seeking.

This can be a shaky and somewhat controversial area. There are numerous people in the world who will argue that they have no control over their feelings. They have been diagnosed with X, and that about covers it for them. Sometimes, a psychotropic drug may offer relief, but for the most part, they are relegated to feeling one way all the time. It is just the curse of being diagnosed with X.

I have a lot of empathy for anyone who feels this way — and not just on a superficial level, either. I suffer from what, at times, feels like a magnetic force field that keeps trying to suck me back into some of the most unhelpful emotions you could imagine. The amount of energy I need to keep myself out of the mud can be exhausting at times. I definitely haven't found a "cure" for this challenge yet. What I have found are some practical techniques for chipping away at these emotions when they appear. These techniques have so far been effective enough to at least shorten their stay, which is a vast improvement over the endless funks that I used to struggle with in my days of using and early recovery.

The Questions We Ask Ourselves

Having lived through a romantic separation recently, I had the opportunity to experience many different emotional states I didn't necessarily appreciate. Whether it was logging onto Facebook and seeing my ex with her new boyfriend or just dealing with the challenge of being alone, I needed to get a handle on my emotions. I found this to be especially important when I first began picking up my daughters on the weekends. In the first few moments we'd be together, I'd be trying to process the feelings of seeing my ex, knowing we were no longer together, and making my kids feel loved and comfortable in this new and foreign situation. It was a lot to reconcile all at once.

If you've been to 12-step meetings, you've heard people speak about their "disease" talking to them in the sound of their own voice or about the endless chatter and noise we have in our heads. Have you ever stopped and thought about what that noise really is? I have.

That noise is usually a ceaseless barrage of questions that we keep asking ourselves. That's essentially what thinking is in the first place, only with the alcoholic and addict brain, the thinking and the questions we ask ourselves are not terribly helpful. Take, for instance, my recent breakup.

The noise in my head was an endless loop of *What's wrong with me? Why does she find him sexier than me? Is this guy going to try to replace me as my kids' father?*

Here's the tricky part, though: it doesn't just come right

out and ask those questions. I, like most people, have a huge ego, and because of this, the noise often comes disguised as *Screw her! They deserve each other. I can do better, anyway.*

But when you peel away all the hubris and bluff, the questions are more sensitive and vulnerable. Either way, when we find ourselves looping the same crappy thoughts over and over, we are basically interrogating ourselves like hapless detectives trying to find answers to questions that have none.

I heard self-help guru Tony Robbins tell a story about a Holocaust survivor named Stanislavsky Lech that forever shaped how I view the questions I ask myself when I am in bad situations. This guy Lech was a prisoner in a Nazi camp, and as he witnessed all the other prisoners around him dying, he noticed that these other guys spent the whole time asking themselves how God could do this to them or why they were in such a horrific situation. Obviously, this was very understandable. If you know much about history, you know that the persecution of Jews by the Nazis was one of the darkest periods of world history.

What Lech was able to figure out, as time went on, was that if he asked himself a different question, he could survive. So, he changed *Why is this happening to me?* to *How can I get out of here?* Now, he was in a concentration camp that was heavily guarded by armed soldiers, so there was no easy answer to this question, but waking up every morning and closing his eyes at night, he kept just repeating that question over and over. Inevitably, he was one of the very few who made it out of that situation alive.

What that story taught me was that the brain is a magical vital organ. We will always get output when we feed it input, and the quality of the output is based primarily on the quality of the input. That's just a fancy way of saying that if we want something good to come out, we need to keep putting good in. So, in my case with my ex-girlfriend, as soon as I realized I was getting trapped in a funk, I began to change the questions I was asking myself, just as Lech did. So, in those first few moments on the weekend when I'd pick up my children, I would change my questions to *How can I make this a good day?* and *What might be positive about their mother and me not being together anymore?*

There was a reason I left that relationship. If I didn't think it was going to improve the quality of my life in some way, there's no way I would have done it. All in all, I was able to get through the hardest days, and like most things, it got easier as time went on.

Pushing Against Resistance

A second useful technique for gaining control over our emotions is, of course, how we use our bodies, or our physiology. I understand that seeing your ex walking down the street arm in arm with your best friend can make it difficult to smile and walk with a swagger in your step, but hear me out: *you have to try to do it anyway.* When you experience less-than-wonderful circumstances, the first thing you want to do is slump your shoulders, put a scowl on your face, and walk like you're headed to the electric chair in one of those old movies from the sixties. Unfortunately, when you allow your body to mourn like that, it only perpetuates more misery. You wind up in a loop of feeling bad and then worse, until you're so far down, you start looking for unhealthy ways to get back up.

So, try this out. Walk around like you're on top of the world, especially if you feel just the opposite. Hold the door for someone, and smile at them, like "I got this" — and guess what, soon you *will* have this. Put your shoulders back and take a deep breath. Keep doing it. Then do it some more. Get up and move around. Moving your body will move your mind. A friend who taught second grade told me that when the kids were stuck on a math problem, she encouraged them to get up and march beside their desks, to switch their brain patterns. You can switch your brain pattern by moving around at any time. Use your body to take you where you want your brain to go — forward.

As difficult as it may sound, you need to push against the inertia of your own sad emotions. Easy? No. Important? Without exaggeration, it is as important as it is to feed yourself and breathe. I'm sure, if you've been to more than one 12-step meeting, you've heard the cliché "Move a muscle, change a thought." I'll be honest: I wanted to punch my sponsor the first time he said that to me. That was not the advice I was looking for, if I remember correctly. All these years later, I finally understand the wisdom in that trope.

One of the most perplexing secrets of life is that the answers we are all looking for are usually in those simple clichés we hear and quickly shrug off, with an "I know" or "No kidding." How do I know this? I used to do the same thing. For decades. When I finally found the secret to making my life incredible, I realized it was because I put all those simple and overused expressions into practice.

I cannot stress this enough. Everyone knows the only way to succeed is to never stop trying, but how many people actually keep trying to accomplish the same thing every morning they wake up — day in, day out for weeks, months, and even sometimes years? Not that many. Just the famous ones you read about in biographies and newspapers.

This is somewhat puzzling, too. I have listened to some of the greatest people of our time give incredible commencement speeches — Jim Carrey, Denzel Washington, J.K. Rowling, Steve Jobs — and the message is generally always the same: Do. Not. Ever. Give. Up. Unfortunately, it's one thing to know something on an intellectual level and another thing entirely to put it into practice. As Edgar Allan Poe mused in his famous story "The Purloined Letter," *sometimes a secret hides in plain sight.*

The Choice to Be Happy

Finally, what we choose to focus on will ultimately determine our emotions. My experience with finishing this book turns out to be a useful example. January and February in the Hudson Valley region of New York can be somewhat brutal. As hard as I push against it, by the middle of February, my mood and morale are almost always dark. It feels as though winter has been going on for an eternity, and more often than not, I even get some kind of bug that puts me down for a few days. Not this winter! This winter I had an entire book to write, and January and February kind of slipped by without my notice. They could have been April and May for all I cared. I was too immersed in what I was doing. It almost makes me feel as if I should probably try to write a book *every* winter.

This is no small thing. I used to dread winter. This year I went to work whistling every day. Snowstorms, icy roads, scraping off my car after work — none of it affected me. I was usually lost in thought about what I was writing, what I had written, or what I was going to write. Now that I realize I have a choice, I will most likely never experience winter the same way again.

I am telling you this not as some great authority but as someone who has just experienced this magical fact firsthand:

what we choose to focus on, how we communicate with ourselves, and how we use our bodies will dictate our feelings and, ultimately, the quality of our lives.

We get to choose. Our circumstances are not that important. They never have been. When you realize this on a visceral level, you, my friend, will have some Kickass Recovery!

CHAPTER TWELVE

Stay High (Frequency)

A re you familiar with the helpful practice of "staying on high frequency," also referred to as "working out in the spiritual gym" or "leaving your car parked in the spiritual garage"? Regardless of what you call it, the result is the same: you maintain your commitment to pushing against the default setting of all humans — the path of least resistance.

It makes sense, too, from a physics standpoint. Former American heavyweight champion boxer Gene Tunney explained that he got his enormous build by pushing against massive weight every single day. He said his muscles "expand by demand."

Life tends to wear us down after a while. Our bosses at work, while we hope they see us as living, breathing humans, will sometimes treat us like we're just a warm body; our lovers will disappoint us from time to time; we'll get speeding tickets. We, too, can only expand by demand.

So, before I bring the curtain down on my dog-and-pony

show, I'd like to leave you with fifty — yes, fifty — ways to stay in spiritual shape over the long haul. Many of them we already covered, of course, but there comes a time when we need a concise review. The end of the book is that time.

1. Read inspirational biographies. If, for some strange reason, you think this will bore you, try doing it for only ten minutes a day. I have a difficult time believing that it could bore anyone, because, honestly, I love reading books like this. Especially audio versions on iBooks, Libro.fm, or Audible when I am working. My favorites are *Steve Jobs* by Walter Isaacson, Stephen King's memoir *On Writing*, Richard Branson's *Losing My Virginity: How I've Survived, Had Fun, and Made a Fortune Doing Business My Way*, and Paul Stanley's *Face the Music: A Life Exposed*. What do I love best about these books? They are real stories about real people with real vision who never gave up in spite of terrible odds.

2. Keep toxic people out of your sphere. While this hardly needs explanation, it may need a little clarification. Toxic people, passive-aggressive people, people who don't believe in you, worry warts, complainers, small thinkers, defeated people — they're everywhere. They're in meetings, at the job, at our dinner table, and sometimes, God forbid, in our cars. Sometimes it is not possible to keep them out of your physical sphere, but for chrissakes, keep them far away from your emotional sphere.

3. Always have a viable plan. You are most likely going to do wondrous things on this planet if you have a clear idea about where you are and an even clearer one about where you're headed. This is, by the way, exactly how a GPS works. Stay grateful for what you have right at this moment, but never lose sight of where you are headed. That attitude worked for me best as I continued to level up.

4. Do something for someone else — every day. First of all, helping others really helps your karma, but more than that, I'm invested in the fact that if we all do this every day, the world will most certainly become a better place to live. On top of that, it's a great antidepressant. A kind gesture releases dopamine in the brain of the giver, the receiver, and anyone who happens to witness the act. That's a lot of dopamine swirling around for the price of your seat on the subway. Or the bus. Or the cable car, if you live in San Francisco.

5. Meditate. Easier said than done, right? Meditation is one of those things people generally drag their feet on, then wonder why they waited so long to try, once they realize what it does for them. I mean, damn, it's right there in the eleventh step of any 12-step program. Studies demonstrate it can make us kinder, less anxious, and less stressed. It has also been shown to decrease blood pressure and improve sleep. For something to have all those benefits and not cost anything, you'd think people everywhere would be doing it all the time. Try it.

6. Never lose sight of the fact that any day could be your last. We all have trouble with this premise. That's fine. It could be paralyzing to spend too much time thinking about our mortality. At the same time, we cannot continually walk around as if we have an infinite amount of time on the planet. Choose your battles wisely. Some things are just not worth getting too worked up over. Chasing someone down and threatening them because they accidentally cut you off in traffic is never an advisable way to spend your time. I mean, for all you know, the woman could have just discovered a breast lump, or the guy might have just found out he's being cheated on. Be kind.

7. Dream big. I mentioned this earlier. There is no difference between you and the people who are doing the big stuff besides the fact that they decided that's what they were going to do. Sound too easy? Put it to the test. Pick any person who is on the so-called top of the world, and figure out how they got there. Nine times out of ten, it's because they *decided* to get there. Everything after that is just logistics.

8. Stay mindful of the story you're telling yourself. Okay, yes, we've touched on this at various times throughout the book, but it bears repeating. There are times this gets tricky. You might find yourself telling everyone in your world how positive you are, then catch yourself thinking, *Here we go again…*, as soon as an obstacle appears in front of you.

Phrases like *Here we go again* indicate that in your deepest soul, you believe life kind of sucks, and now you have more proof of that. If you notice yourself doing that — stop! The Seven-Day Mental Positivity Diet that I talked about in chapter 10 can help you with this.

9. You are in charge of what reality is — so make it good. As I said, our circumstances really don't have as much to do with our reality as we think. It's what we focus on, how we carry ourselves, and our self-talk that really run the show. You are in control of all those things. If you were invited to a party at someone's palatial estate and you spent the entire time by the bar where people were getting drunk and arguing all night, you'd say the party was horrible and all everyone was doing was fighting. This would be completely wrong. Somewhere on the third floor, two people were falling in love and kissing passionately. Out by the guesthouse, someone else was doing magic tricks for the kids, and by the pool, a very wealthy businessman just offered a life-changing job to the server who was broke. In other words, don't judge the whole of life by the one room you're staring into. It's a big world. Focus on what's good.

10. Listen to an inspirational podcast every day. There are some incredible ones out there right now. Some are archived short series, like *Making Oprah* and *Making Obama*, and some are classics, like *This American Life, Heavyweight, The Moth, Thank You Heartbreak,* and *Hidden Brain*, that still drop every week. Some are slick productions, like *Radiolab*, and some will bring you to tears, like *Modern Love*. These podcasts are so much more than entertainment. They evoke emotion, they inspire, they teach, and they enrich lives. If you haven't tried them, now's the time. You'll be glad you did.

11. Don't compare yourself with others. Now, don't confuse this with the useful envy I brought up in chapter 6, "Find Your Calling." As I mentioned, it can be helpful to use the envy you feel when you see others doing what you would like to do to propel you in the direction you seek. But it's detrimental to feel inferior around the guy with the new Corvette when you have a two-year-old Honda Civic, or to feel like someone has a hotter boyfriend or a better job. These things are subjective, and they drive us crazy if we let them.

12. Stay off social media as much as possible. Speaking of comparing yourself with others, Facebook, Instagram, and Twitter were designed to give you a PhD in looking at other people and feeling sorry for yourself. It's all hype. You know it is. For many of us, it is a necessary evil. Sometimes if we want to know what distant family members are up to or promote our blogs, we need to use it. *Helpful hint: take it off your phone.* That way, you only look at it on your laptop or desktop, and you don't obsessively check your notifications 450 times a day. Once again, I say this from firsthand experience. I noticed a complete change in my morale when I deleted Facebook from my phone.

13. Eat well. I'm not trying to sound like your mother, but processed crap makes up about 95 percent of everything edible in convenience stores, truck stops, and rest areas. I am kind of a sucker for pizza and burritos, so if I spot one of those places along the way, I always get something. The way I balance this out is by packing my cooler full of fruit, vegetables, and granola every day. I make sure that my ratio of garbage to good stuff is about one to four. I don't plan on trying to market this as the Manas Diet, but essentially, use your head. Keep an eye on the amount of poison you ingest.

14. Sleep enough. Have you ever noticed how little kids start acting irrational and loony tunes just before they pass out in the car? There's some science behind this phenomenon. Sleep deprivation causes depression, irritability, decreased cognitive capacity, and moodiness. Over time, it lowers your immunity and makes you more susceptible to colds and the flu. In short, life feels a lot better when you get enough sleep. Balance is key, though. Too much sleep can make you lethargic and unmotivated. Six to eight hours is optimal for most people.

15. Drink plenty of water. We've all heard, "Drink eight 8-ounce glasses of water every day for optimal health" — this instruction really doesn't have any basis in fact. Your best bet is to make sure you are drinking enough to stay hydrated. It's the only way to keep the toxins flushed out of your body.

16. Avoid meat when possible. If you're a vegan or a vegetarian, great. If not, I would never expect you to change that now; however, in the United States the average person eats about two hundred pounds of meat every year. It's a bit much. In countries with fewer resources, the populations eat more vegetables and generally experience fewer cases of heart disease and cancer per capita. Definitely something to at least consider.

17. Avoid sugar when possible. This can be harder than staying away from double cheeseburgers — I get it. As a former sweets enthusiast, I have to tell you that when I gradually decreased white sugar from my diet, things really began to improve for me. Most processed foods have added sugar these days, so you might be ingesting a lot more than you realize. It's something to be mindful of. A helpful new hobby might be to read food labels.

18. Avoid fast food at all costs. Like many of the other things I've mentioned, if you're going to be out there hustling, and most especially if you're getting into the world of trucking, this is going to take a little doing, but it's not entirely impossible. It does take some effort. You're going to be shuttling as fast as you can from city to city, oftentimes with only ten hours between fourteen-hour driving shifts, and sometimes you just want a burger, fries, and your blanket. Totally understandable. If it becomes an everyday habit, you'll regret it. Make the effort to take care of yourself.

19. Stay optimistic no matter what. When you are optimistic, it is contagious. Given that you have the choice of spreading good vibes or bad vibes, why wouldn't you choose good? Optimism also keeps people expansive and curious. So much so that nothing in this entire book is going to be of any use if you don't approach it with positivity. I can't count how many times I've said this, but you create your own reality. If you see things as shitty, guess how things are going to be? Case closed.

20. Do at least one thing to move yourself forward every day. And I mean anything — even small actions that take a minute, like making a phone call or reading a page on a website about a skill you want to learn. First of all, there's the pragmatic aspect to doing this. We make enormous changes incrementally, so each day you obviously need to add some kind of increment. In a holistic sense, though, when you are looking for something each day to get you from A to B, you are sending a signal to your subconscious that you are heading in a purposeful direction. With that information in your subconscious, you won't fall victim to feelings of stagnation or hopelessness, and you'll create a general sense of contentment inside yourself. It's a win-win.

21. Go to a meeting. I have a friend who works on the front lines of the opioid epidemic every day. She's the one who shows up after someone's been revived by Narcan to suggest various ways for the patient to get help. She is a solution-based person who sees 12-step meetings as being statistically ineffectual — meaning, the success rate is low. People relapse. People die. Not being a narrow-minded person, I do not argue with her. There is something to be said for her point of view; however, for me and a lot of the people I've come to love, NA and AA are what stand between us and certain death. These groups saved us from isolation and gave us a network of support that usually can't be found on a typical suboxone or methadone program. However you feel about this issue, there is something great that happens in those rooms, so give it a shot. I would not be writing this without the love and support of the people in those programs.

22. Stay away from negative music. Seriously, who doesn't love rockin' out to classic Jay-Z, Eminem, and even a little death metal here and there? Unfortunately, evoking a constant flow of imagery of shooting people, robbing people, putting women down, and acting shitty to everyone around us doesn't do much for our overall outlook. A famous 2015 study done at three different universities in Finland went deep with this, but let's keep it short and sweet: bad music gives you bad feelings.

23. Wake up early whenever you can. It is 6:23 AM on a Saturday at this very moment. Part of what keeps me doing the seemingly impossible — like, say, writing an entire book in two months, while working sixty hours a week as a truck driver — is that the snooze button and I have never been formally introduced. When most people's alarms are going off, I've already written one thousand words, showered, dressed, and read something inspiring. You might say it's the secret to my success.

24. Call your sponsor. Of course, if that's not your thing, call another supportive person, someone to bounce ideas off of, someone who believes in you. In the hard-and-fast rules of *the* program, this is not exactly what a sponsor is supposed to be for, but it's what a sponsor has always been for me. Stay close with whoever supports you in the great challenge of staying clean and sober.

25. Stay in a place of gratitude. It's practically impossible to be grouchy when you start your day by realizing how lucky you are to be alive and surrounded by people you love and who love you right back. If that weren't enough, we also live in a place where we are free to become whatever we can imagine and dream up, free to read whatever we want, and free to roam around wherever we have a mind to. When you are rooted in a place of gratitude, you are coming from a position of power. When you are whiny and ungrateful, you are coming from a place of helplessness. Choose wisely.

26. Exercise. Tony Robbins has this thing called "The Hour of Power," "Thirty Minutes to Thrive," and "Fifteen Minutes for Fulfillment," where he takes the combination of exercise and gratitude and turns it into a shot of superpower every morning. If you're interested, you can google it. With my schedule, fifteen minutes on a rebounder, staring at my vision board and thinking about everyone I love gets me buzzing with excitement every day.

27. Talk to a newcomer. This is also related to 12-step recovery, because frankly, outside of a meeting, it's difficult to know if you're talking to a committed newcomer or someone who just hasn't used in a few hours. Either way, it's proved that sharing our recovery strengthens our recovery. Share yours whenever possible.

28. Learn to steer clear of bullshit. This means *any and all* bullshit. If you start dating someone who has endless issues with their ex, run for your life. If you have endless problems with *your* ex, just stop already. I understand that some stuff — for instance, family court — can be unavoidable. Be reasonable about it, though. Are there other places where bullshit exists that you can possibly avoid? If so, get to it. Life is short.

29. Do something nice for yourself every day. This doesn't even have to be elaborate. Take a few minutes and think of how incredible you are for reading this book and committing to a better life. Look in the mirror and remind yourself how ridiculously beautiful you are. Or buy yourself a chocolate-covered cherry. It all works. (I realize number 17 says to stay away from sugar, but I mean, come on — you don't have to be an extremist.)

30. Share at a meeting like your life depends on it. I'm a big fan of this part of 12-step meetings. There is no other medicine on the planet quite like raising your hand in that room full of people and letting it all hang out. I'm certain it has saved my life on occasion. Every so often, when the going gets tough, remember that sharing at a meeting is always available to you.

31. Don't forget that if you are reading this book…you are ten steps ahead of most everyone else. As a matter of fact, studies show that less than 25 percent of those who attempt to turn over a new leaf, make New Year's resolutions, or join a gym actually stay committed for longer than a month. Bask for a minute in the fact that you are one of the few and the proud.

32. Keep your space clean and organized. There's a reason Admiral William H. McRaven's famous commencement speech at the University of Texas at Austin has over 9 million views on YouTube. It's damn good advice. "If you're looking to change the world," he says, "start by making your bed. You will have completed one small task, and it will encourage you to complete another one. You can't expect to do the big things right if you ignore the small things."

33. Time is money — spend it wisely. Sometimes when we have free time — say, for example, on a day off — we'll realize we have spent hours either scrolling through Facebook, binge-watching *Real Housewives of New Jersey*, or screening cat videos on YouTube. Time can be tricky. When we are spaced-out, it seems like it goes on forever, but believe me: our time here is short. Use it wisely.

34. Buy art — even cheap stuff — and hang it on your wall. I can think of two great reasons for this: When you have interesting things decorating your space, it stimulates your own creativity. More importantly, though, there are a lot of great unknown artists who can sure use the encouragement and the bread. Make someone smile and help yourself in the process. What? You don't live in a town with a liberal-arts college or street fairs on a regular basis? No problem. Log on to Etsy. You can find plenty of prints and paintings for ten dollars.

35. If you have kids, cherish them. Try this: take your kids to the bounce house and shut off your phone. They'll really appreciate it, and you will have a totally different experience. Take them to the diner. Don't have twenty bucks? Take them on a hike or a walk down the block. Referring back to number 33, life is short and time with your children is precious. You can wait until they go to bed to watch that video of the exploding cantaloupe.

36. Call an old friend. I realize this is controversial advice in this day and age. We've reached a point where unscheduled phone calls have become an almost invasive form of communication. So, by all means, let them know via Messenger you'll be reaching out, if you have to. When I'm feeling a little off my game, nothing makes me feel human again like a call to an old friend.

37. Forgive someone. You know that person you said you'd never forgive? Forgive them. That doesn't necessarily mean you're giving the offending party a pass or even that you are continuing a relationship with them. Anger and resentment are far more toxic to you than they could ever be to the other person. Don't allow yourself to be defined by useless emotions. Let it go and forgive.

38. Turn off the TV. It's a terrible time-suck, it wreaks havoc on your cognitive ability, it's been proved to lower people's quality of life, it's mostly negative, it makes people believe the world is way worse than it actually is — and if those are not enough reasons, the fact that it just plain sucks should be more than sufficient.

39. Go to the library and pick out something awesome to read. Like one of those great biographies I told you about. Or something by Brené Brown or Pema Chödrön that will make you feel good about yourself. Now that you're not watching FOX News anymore, you'll have plenty of time for it, too.

40. Let go of some bullshit. Did anyone ever stand you up? Cheat on you? Exclude you from something? Make you feel "less than"? Don't let it hang on you like a rusty iron anchor, because when all is said and done, by next year you won't even remember. Why even wait for a year? Forget about it right now.

41. Spend a minute every day congratulating yourself for being sober. It can be easy, as we get more and more time away from active addiction, to forget about how bad things were. This is understandable. Who likes to spend their time dredging up bad memories? Unfortunately, if we don't spend a little time remembering, it can be fatal. Remember where you were then. Take stock of where you are now. Congratulate yourself.

42. Compliment someone. I'm real big on small acts of kindness — especially these days, when the social and political climate seems somewhere between WTF and batshit crazy. Take a second, notice something positive about someone else, and let them know. Besides, if you're having a miserable day, it will take the focus off you for a minute, and that could be exactly what you need.

43. Stay out of arguments. This goes double for Facebook and Twitter battles. Nothing will drag you below the surface faster than arguing with trolls about which president created more jobs or tanked the economy. It has to be one of the lowest-frequency activities on the planet. If you get worked up about something you see online that is patently false, yell about it — but keep your fingers in your pocket.

44. Write a thank-you note. We've reached a place in our society where a little thing like a thank-you note has become antiquated and quaint, but if you want to turn *gratitude* into an actual verb, I can't think of a better way. The small effort of sitting down with pen and paper and gifting the person who has been there for you with a keepsake can pay off big in the long run. They'll feel appreciated, and you'll feel good about yourself.

45. Fix something that needs fixing. This is something my first sponsor used to refer to as an "esteemable act," and anything that helps build self-esteem is worth doing. It can be any fix-it, from a broken shower knob that drives you crazy every morning to a loose hinge on the door to your bedroom. The sense of accomplishment you'll feel afterward will have you walking on air a little bit each time you see that it's no longer broken.

46. If you notice yourself complaining…stop! Not only is complaining a low-frequency activity, but it is very bad for your health. Recent research done at Stanford University has proved that constant complaining can actually result in shrinking the part of the brain known as the hippocampus. The hippocampus is where problem solving and long-term memory storage take place, and it's also one of the first areas affected by Alzheimer's disease. If all that weren't enough, the act of complaining has also been shown to release extra cortisol in your body, and that *will* break down your immune system eventually. Besides that, how often do you hear people say, "Let's go sit by Yolanda! I love how she complains about everything all the time"?

47. Laugh. In 1964, following a stressful trip to Russia, author Norman Cousins came back to the States with a rare illness called ankylosing spondylitis. In a nutshell, it's a degenerative disease that breaks down the body's collagen and results in excruciating pain. His doctors advised him he'd probably die within a few months' time. Cousins had a feeling that if stress caused the disease, laughter could cure it. With his doctors' permission, he checked himself out of the hospital, got a hotel room across the street, and spent hours watching old episodes of *Candid Camera* and Marx Brothers movies. He noticed that at one point he was laughing so hard, he grew tired and got his first two hours of uninterrupted, pain-free sleep since becoming ill. Over time, he cured himself with this method, and spurred numerous studies on the effect of laughter on the body. Spend a little time laughing every day.

48. Let go of something that doesn't serve you. To paraphrase a Buddhist philosopher from the fifth century, anger is like picking up a pile of dog crap and trying to throw it on someone. You'll most likely miss, and your hand is going to stink. Let it go. Leave the dog crap on the ground where it belongs.

49. Don't lie. The average person tells about eleven lies every week. Researchers at the University of Notre Dame began with this premise when they tracked people's health, and found that lying less cut down on headaches, stomachaches, and stress. If you can avoid lying every day, you could be as healthy and strong as an ox. Or at the very least, just be known as someone who isn't a bullshitter. Either one is reason enough, yes?

50. Love yourself. This needs no explanation.

Remember this: the fact that you are not using and not drinking makes you a medical anomaly right from the jump. You have every reason in the world to walk around with your head held high, your chest out, and a big ol' grin on your face. The fact that you even *want* to create a more compelling life for yourself means you're halfway there. Most people don't really go beyond the wishing stage.

No one can deny that having a beautiful family, a new car, a great job, and a hot crib is badass. But it's what you become on the way to making all that happen that is most important.

You'll expand who you *are* so far beyond who you *were* when you were out there struggling.

You won't even recognize yourself anymore.

You are so much more than a person in recovery.

You are a rockstar!

Epilogue

I f you've ever had the pleasure of reading Anthony Bourdain's *Kitchen Confidential*, you might remember that, chapter after chapter, he laid down all the rules of what works in the real world of restaurant management and what always fails. Then, at the end, he introduces the chef Scott Bryan from the restaurant Veritas and slowly recounts how almost everything he established as hard-and-fast rules in the first three-quarters of the book is not always true. "The whole world of cooking is not my world, contrary to what impression I might have given you in the preceding pages," Bourdain writes. "Truth be told, I bring a lot of it with me. Hang out in the Veritas kitchen, take a hard look at Scott Bryan's operation, and you will find that everything I've told you so far is wrong, that all my sweeping generalities, rules of thumb, preconceptions and general principles are utter bullshit."

Of course, he was being ironic and somewhat humorous.

Most of what he conveyed in his book was true. Scott Bryan and his business partner, Gino Diaferia, were obviously an anomaly. An exception.

I bring this up because the passage struck a chord with me. Nothing is true 100 percent of the time. As for my book, if most people apply the principles that I've laid out, they too can have the beautiful, fulfilling life that I've come to know and love. They can create a compelling and interesting world for themselves and enjoy all the great things they missed out on while they were a slave to getting drugs, using drugs, and finding the ways and means to get more drugs.

Unfortunately, relapse is always a possibility. If you've ever listened to or even heard of the podcast *Dopey*, you know that it defies almost everything I have said in the last couple of hundred pages. Here were two guys, Dave and Chris, who met at a rehab, got sober, started a podcast, and experienced great success. To take it a step further, Chris went on to live with the kind of girlfriend dreams are made of, was enrolled in medical school, and for all intents and purposes was staring right down the barrel at an incredible future. That is, until he relapsed and subsequently overdosed and died shortly after the 142nd episode.

His relapse was, sadly, the kind of story we hear often in the rooms of 12-step programs. He injured himself, he was prescribed painkillers, it roused the sleeping monster that lives inside all of us, and — bam! — he was off to the races. What makes it even spookier is that on the hundredth episode, Chris practically predicted the steps that led to his own demise: "One of us will get injured, get pain meds, and take them while doing *Dopey*." To be honest, when you listen, you can tell that the possibility of it leading to death never crossed his mind.

Not that Dave and Chris were in denial about how often

people die: one of their recurring guests and very close friends, Todd — whom Dave was hoping to make a cohost — relapsed and died shortly after getting out of a sober-living house. But you know how it is with most people: death is something that only happens to the other guy. I am not saying that in a flippant way; it's just one of the existential aspects of being human.

What I'm trying to say is that I hope this book will help you. I hope it will awaken things in you that lead you to go on and become bigger than you've ever imagined you could be. I know these principles did that for me. But keep in mind that all any of us get is a daily reprieve. For most of us, that is enough. For some, it isn't. That is the brutal truth about drug and alcohol addiction. As it says in the Basic Text of Narcotics Anonymous, this disease is *cunning, baffling, and insidious.* For every success story, there's a tragic tale of a life cut short. Sometimes there are no words of wisdom besides these: be careful out there.

Acknowledgments

First and foremost, I'd like to thank Linda Konner for believing in me. Then I have to thank Georgia Hughes; Kate Hanley, without whom none of this would be possible; Larry Ruhl; Kristin Nimsger, for helping me believe in myself; Kitty Sheehan; Pavita Singh; Crystal Jackson; Yoli Ramazzina; Christina Moffett, for being the baddest coach a guy could have; and, of course, Liberty DeVitto for being Liberty DeVitto.

Directory of State Vocational Rehabilitation Agencies

The information in this list is current as of fall 2019. Each listing below has the phone number for the central or administrative office. However, the websites for many states' programs include phone numbers for local offices, so you might have better luck if you go to the website first and search for the office in your area. Good luck!

ALABAMA
Department of Rehabilitation Services
Phone: (334) 293-7500 • Toll-Free: (800) 441-7607
Website: http://www.rehab.alabama.gov

ALASKA
Division of Vocational Rehabilitation
Phone: (907) 465-2814 • Toll-Free: (800) 478-2815
Website: http://labor.alaska.gov/dvr/home.htm

ARIZONA
Rehabilitation Services Administration
Toll-Free: (800) 563-1221
Website: https://www.azdes.gov/RSA

ARKANSAS
Rehabilitation Services Division
Phone: (501) 296-1600 • Toll-Free: (800) 330-0632
Website: https://www.arcareereducation.org/about/arkansas
   -rehabilitation-services

CALIFORNIA
Department of Rehabilitation
Phone: (916) 324-1313 • Toll-Free: (800) 952-5544
Website: https://www.dor.ca.gov

COLORADO
Division of Vocational Rehabilitation
Phone: (303) 318-8571
Website: https://www.colorado.gov/dvr

CONNECTICUT
Bureau of Rehabilitation Services
Toll-Free: (800) 537-2549
Website: https://portal.ct.gov/AgingandDisability/Content-Pages
   /Bureaus/Bureau-of-Rehabilitation-Services

DELAWARE
Division of Vocational Rehabilitation
Phone: (302) 761-8275
Website: https://dvr.delawareworks.com

DISTRICT OF COLUMBIA
Vocational Rehabilitation Services
Phone: (202) 730-1700
Website: https://dds.dc.gov/service/vocational-rehabilitation-services

FLORIDA
Division of Vocational Rehabilitation
Phone: (850) 245-3399 • Toll-Free: (800) 451-4327
Website: http://www.rehabworks.org

GEORGIA
Georgia Vocational Rehabilitation Agency
Phone: (844) 367-4872
Website: https://gvs.georgia.gov/vocational-rehabilitation

HAWAII
Vocational and Rehabilitation Agency
Phone: (808) 586-9729
Website: http://humanservices.hawaii.gov/vr

IDAHO
Division of Vocational Rehabilitation
Phone: (208) 334-3390
Website: http://www.vr.idaho.gov

ILLINOIS
Division of Rehabilitation Services
Toll-Free: (800) 843-6154
Website: http://www.dhs.state.il.us/page.aspx?item=29736

INDIANA
Vocational Rehabilitation Services
Toll-Free: (800) 545-7763
Website: https://www.in.gov/fssa/ddrs/2636.htm

IOWA
Vocational Rehabilitation Services
Phone: (515) 281-4211 • Toll-Free: (800) 532-1486
Website: http://www.ivrs.iowa.gov

KANSAS
Vocational Rehabilitation Services
Phone: 785-368-7471 • Toll-Free: 1-866-213-9079
Website: http://www.dcf.ks.gov/services/RS/Pages/Employment
   -Services.aspx

KENTUCKY
Office of Vocational Rehabilitation
Toll-Free: (800) 372-7172
Website: https://kcc.ky.gov/Vocational-Rehabilitation

LOUISIANA
Vocational Rehabilitation Program
Phone: (225) 219-2225 • Toll-Free: (800) 737-2958
Website: http://www.laworks.net/WorkforceDev/LRS/LRS
   _Rehabilitation.asp

MAINE
Division of Vocational Rehabilitation
Phone: (207) 623-6799
Website: https://www.maine.gov/rehab/dvr/vr.shtml

MARYLAND
Division of Rehabilitation Services
Phone: (410) 554-9442 • Toll-Free: (888) 554-0334
Website: https://dors.maryland.gov

MASSACHUSETTS

Massachusetts Rehabilitation Commission Vocational Rehabilitation
Phone: (617) 204-3600
Website: https://www.mass.gov/vocational-rehabilitation

MICHIGAN

Vocational Rehabilitation
Phone: (517) 241-5324 • Toll-Free: (800) 605-6722
Website: https://www.michigan.gov/leo/0,5863,7-336-78421_95508
_26929---,00.html

MINNESOTA

Vocational Rehabilitation Services
Phone: (651) 259-7114
Website: https://mn.gov/deed/job-seekers/disabilities

MISSISSIPPI

Office of Vocational Rehabilitation
Toll-Free: (800) 443-1000
Website: https://www.mdrs.ms.gov/VocationalRehab

MISSOURI

Division of Vocational Rehabilitation
Phone: (573) 751-3251 • Toll-Free: (877) 222-8963
Website: http://dese.mo.gov/vr

MONTANA

Vocational Rehabilitation
Phone: (406) 444-2590 • Toll-Free: (877) 296-1197
Website: http://www.dphhs.mt.gov/detd/vocrehab

NEBRASKA
Vocational Rehabilitation
Phone: (402) 471-3644 • Toll-Free: (877) 637-3422
Website: http://vr.nebraska.gov

NEVADA
Rehabilitation Division
Northern Nevada — Phone: (775) 687-6860
Southern Nevada — Phone: (702) 486-5230
Website: https://detr.nv.gov/Page/Rehabilitation_Division_Bureau_of
_Vocational_Rehabilitation

NEW HAMPSHIRE
Vocational Rehabilitation
Phone: (603) 271-3471 • Toll-Free: (800) 299-1647
Website: http://www.education.nh.gov/career/vocational

NEW JERSEY
Vocational Rehabilitation Services
Phone: (609) 292-5987
Website: https://careerconnections.nj.gov/careerconnections/plan
/foryou/disable/vocational_rehabilitation_services.shtml

NEW MEXICO
Division of Vocational Rehabilitation
Phone: (505) 954-8500 • Toll-Free: (800) 224-7005
Website: http://www.dvr.state.nm.us

NEW YORK
ACCES-VR — Vocational Rehabilitation
Toll-Free: (800) 222-JOBS (5627)
Website: http://www.acces.nysed.gov/vr

NORTH CAROLINA

Vocational Rehabilitation Services

Phone: (919) 855-3500 • Toll-Free: (800) 689-9090

Website: http://dvr.dhhs.state.nc.us

NORTH DAKOTA

Vocational Rehabilitation

Phone: (701) 328-8950 • Toll-Free: (800) 755-2745

Website: http://www.nd.gov/dhs/dvr/index.html

OHIO

Bureau of Vocational Rehabilitation

Phone: (614) 438-1200 • Toll-Free: (800) 282-4536

Website: https://ood.ohio.gov/Services/Vocational-Rehabilitation

OKLAHOMA

Vocational Rehabilitation

Phone: (405) 951-3470 • Toll-Free: (800) 845-8476

Website: http://www.okrehab.org/job-seekers/dvr

OREGON

Vocational Rehabilitation

Phone: (503) 945-5880 • Toll-Free: (877) 277-0513

Website: http://www.oregon.gov/DHS/vr/

PENNSYLVANIA

Vocational Rehabilitation Services

Phone: (717) 787-5244 • Toll-Free: (800) 442-6351

Website: https://www.dli.pa.gov/Individuals/Disability-Services/ovr
/Pages/default.aspx

RHODE ISLAND

Vocational Rehabilitation Program

Phone: (401) 421-7005

Website: http://www.ors.ri.gov/VR.html

SOUTH CAROLINA
Vocational Rehabilitation Department
Phone: (803) 896-6500 • Toll-Free: (800) 832-7526
Website: http://www.scvrd.net

SOUTH DAKOTA
Vocational Rehabilitation
Phone: (605) 773-3195 or (605) 773-6412
Website: https://dhs.sd.gov/rehabservices/vr.aspx

TENNESSEE
Vocational Rehabilitation
Phone: (615) 313-4891
Website: https://www.tn.gov/humanservices/ds/vocational
-rehabilitation.html

TEXAS
Vocational Rehabilitation Services
Toll-Free: (800) 628-5115
Website: https://twc.texas.gov/jobseekers/vocational-rehabilitation
-services

UTAH
Vocational Rehabilitation
Toll-Free: (866) 454-8397
Website: https://jobs.utah.gov/usor/vr

VERMONT
Division of Vocational Rehabilitation
Toll-Free: (866) 879-6757
Website: http://vocrehab.vermont.gov

VIRGINIA
Vocational Rehabilitation Program
Toll-Free: (800) 552-5019
Website: https://www.vadars.org/drs/vr/

WASHINGTON
Division of Vocational Rehabilitation
Phone: (206) 273-7100 • Toll-Free: (800) 622-1375
Website: http://www.dshs.wa.gov/dvr

WEST VIRGINIA
Division of Rehabilitation Services
Phone: (304) 356-2060 • Toll-Free: (800) 642-8207
Website: http://www.wvdrs.org

WISCONSIN
Vocational Rehabilitation
Phone: (608) 261-0050 • Toll-Free: (800) 442-3477
Website: http://dwd.wisconsin.gov/dvr

WYOMING
Vocational Rehabilitation
Phone: (307) 777-7386
Website: http://wyomingworkforce.org/workers/vr

Territories

AMERICAN SAMOA
Division of Vocational Rehabilitation
Phone: (684) 699-1371
Website: http://www.dhss.as

GUAM

Division of Vocational Rehabilitation
Phone: (671) 475-5735
Website: http://disid.guam.gov/division-of-vocational-rehabilitation/

NORTHERN MARIANA ISLANDS

Office of Vocational Rehabilitation
Phone: (670) 322-6537
Website: http://www.ovrgov.net

PUERTO RICO

Administración de Rehabilitación Vocacional
Phone: (787) 729-0160
Website: http://www.arv.pr.gov/Pages/default.aspx

VIRGIN ISLANDS

Division of Disabilities and Rehabilitation Services
Phone: (340) 774-0930
Website: http://www.dhs.gov.vi/disabilities/index.html

Endnotes

Chapter Two: Name Your *Why*

p. 29   *I remember hearing the story of Lisa Erspamer:* Lisa Erspamer, *Making Oprah* podcast, episode 3, "You Get a Car," November 22, 2016, https://www.wbez.org/series/making-oprah/db4fff18 -4828-4589-b03f-8dd50a5adbbe.

Chapter Six: Find Your Calling

p. 79   *It is what author and speaker Kyle Cease referred to as "living from the inside out":* Kyle Cease, "Why People's Opinions of You Aren't Real," September 27, 2015, 4:21, YouTube video, https://www.youtube.com/watch?v=qkdq1-vOwHA.

p. 81   *The "Morning Pages," an exercise in which you write stream-of-consciousness style:* Julia Cameron, *The Artist's Way: A Spiritual Path to Higher Creativity — 25th Anniversary Edition* (1992; reprint, New York: TarcherPerigee, 2016), 9.

Chapter Seven: Rehearse Happiness

p. 88   *Olympic coach Dr. Richard Suinn discovered:* Rick Maese, "For Olympians, Seeing (in Their Minds) Is Believing (It Can Happen)," *Washington Post,* July 28, 2016, https://www.washington post.com/sports/olympics/for-olympians-seeing-in-their-minds -is-believing-it-can-happen/2016/07/28/6966709c-532e-11e6 -bbf5-957ad17b4385_story.html.

p. 88   *A genius named Dr. Joe Dispenza made a lifelong study:* Dr. Joe Dispenza, *Breaking the Habit of Being Yourself: How to Lose Your Mind and Create a New One* (Carlsbad, CA: Hay House, 2012).

p. 91   *"Produce it anyway," Ford said:* Napoleon Hill, *Think and Grow Rich* (1937; reprint, Shippensburg, PA: Sound Wisdom / Napoleon Hill Foundation, 2017), 31.

p. 92   *When Edison struggled to invent the lightbulb:* "Myth Busters: Edison's 1,000 Attempts," *The Edisonian,* vol. 9, fall 2012, Thomas A. Edison papers, Rutgers School of Arts and Sciences, https://edison.rutgers.edu/newsletter9.html

p. 92   *"Why, man, I have gotten lots of results! I know several thousand things that won't work!":* Frank Lewis Dyer and Thomas Commerford Martin, *Edison: His Life and Inventions,* vol. 2 (1910; reprint, Honolulu: University Press of the Pacific, 2001), 616.

p. 93   *Colonel Sanders received his first Social Security check for $105:* William Whitworth, "Kentucky Fried," *New Yorker,* February 6, 1970, https://www.newyorker.com/magazine/1970/02/14 /kentucky-fried.

Chapter Nine: Create an Environment of Success

p. 116   *"put things in their places":* Benjamin Franklin, *The Life of Benjamin Franklin,* vol. 1, ed. John Bigelow (Philadelphia: Lippincott, 1875), 237.

Chapter Ten: Prepare for Takeoff

p. 133   *Robbins decided that we needed an American phrase:* Tony Robbins, *Awaken the Giant Within: How to Take Immediate Control of Your Mental, Emotional, Physical & Financial Destiny* (1991; reprint, New York: Simon & Schuster, 2003), 214.

Chapter Eleven: Seal Off the Exits

p. 142 *I landed on an interview with Jim Carrey:* "Jim Carrey about His Dad," YouTube video, December 13, 2017, 2:06, https://www.youtube.com/watch?v=gC8XJenmURY.

p. 143 *Statistically speaking, 80 percent of them have given up by February 15:* Joseph Luciani, "Why 80 Percent of New Year's Resolutions Fail," *U.S. News & World Report*, December 29, 2015, https://health.usnews.com/health-news/blogs/eat-run/articles/2015-12-29/why-80-percent-of-new-years-resolutions-fail.

p. 149 *Holocaust survivor named Stanislavsky Lech*: Tony Robbins, *Awaken the Giant Within: How to Take Immediate Control of Your Mental, Emotional, Physical & Financial Destiny* (1991; reprint, New York: Simon & Schuster, 2003), 177–79.

Chapter Twelve: Stay High (Frequency)

p. 155 *He said his muscles "expand by demand":* Dr. Dennis Buckley, "Expand by Demand," *Mountain Views News*, January 19, 2013, http://www.mtnviewsnews.com/v07/htm/n03/p11.htm.

p. 165 *William H. McRaven's famous commencement speech:* Admiral William H. McRaven, "University of Texas at Austin 2014 Commencement Address," May 19, 2014, YouTube video, 19:26, https://www.youtube.com/watch?v=pxBQLFLei7o.

p. 168 *Norman Cousins came back to the States with a rare illness:* Norman Cousins, *Anatomy of an Illness: As Perceived by the Patient* (New York: Norton, 1979).

Epilogue

p. 171 *"The whole world of cooking...":* Anthony Bourdain, *Kitchen Confidential: Adventures in the Culinary Underbelly* (London: Bloomsbury Publishing, 2000), 252–53.

About the Author

B illy Manas is a columnist for *Elephant Journal*, a contributor to *The Good Men Project*, a published poet, and a
twenty-year veteran singer-songwriter who plays eighty-plus
gigs a year throughout the Hudson Valley.

Manas wasn't always this prolific — for over two decades
he lived the life of an addict. Not a living-in-the-gutter, pan-
handling addict but a methadone-swilling, Adderall-chewing,
weed-smoking, never-miss-a-gig addict.

Fortunately, in 2010, when he realized mortality was staring him in the face and laughing, Manas gave Narcotics Anonymous one more attempt and has stayed clean ever since. Now
he uses all that creativity and those scrounging skills to earn
$1,000 a week as a truck driver, raise two young daughters
(ages three and five) as a single father, and help others trapped
by substance abuse create compelling lives for themselves.

Manas's artistic efforts have been featured in the *Woodstock
Times*, the *Hudson Valley Almanac*, and the *Poughkeepsie Jour-
nal*. His poetry has appeared in *Mused* magazine and *Elephant
Journal*, and he has performed music live on Q92 FM, WPDH,
WVKR, and WDST. For more info, visit billymanas.com.

NEW WORLD LIBRARY is dedicated to publishing books and other media that inspire and challenge us to improve the quality of our lives and the world.

We are a socially and environmentally aware company. We recognize that we have an ethical responsibility to our readers, our authors, our staff members, and our planet.

We serve our readers by creating the finest publications possible on personal growth, creativity, spirituality, wellness, and other areas of emerging importance. We serve our authors by working with them to produce and promote quality books that reach a wide audience. We serve New World Library employees with generous benefits, significant profit sharing, and constant encouragement to pursue their most expansive dreams.

Whenever possible, we print our books with soy-based ink on 100 percent postconsumer-waste recycled paper. We power our offices with solar energy and contribute to nonprofit organizations working to make the world a better place for us all.

Our products are available wherever books are sold. Visit our website to download our catalog, subscribe to our e-newsletter, read our blog, and link to authors' websites, videos, and podcasts.

customerservice@newworldlibrary.com
Phone: 415-884-2100 or 800-972-6657
Orders: Ext. 10 • Catalog requests: Ext. 10
Fax: 415-884-2199

www.newworldlibrary.com